REAL SQL QUERIES
50 CHALLENGES
SECOND EDITION

Brian Cohen

Neil Pepi

Neerja Mishra

Real SQL Queries: 50 Challenges
By Brian Cohen, Neil Pepi, and Neerja Mishra

© 2015, 2017 Brian Cohen, Neil Pepi, and Neerja Mishra.

ISBN-10: 1979935017
ISBN-13: 978-1979935012

All rights reserved. No part of this book may be reproduced or transmitted in any form or by any means, electronic, mechanical, photocopying, recording, or otherwise, without prior written permission of the authors.

Microsoft, Excel, and SQL Server are either registered trademarks or trademarks of Microsoft Corporation in the United States and/or other countries. All other trademarks are the property of their respective owners. When trademark designations appear in this book, and the authors were aware of a trademark claim, the designations have been printed in initial capital letters.

While every precaution has been taken in the preparation of this book, the authors assume no responsibility for errors or omissions, or for damages resulting from the use or information contained herein.

Copy Editor: Haley DeLeon

Publication History:
August 2015 – eBook First Edition
December 2015 – Paperback First Edition
November 2017 – eBook Second Edition
November 2017 – Paperback Second Edition

Second Edition feedback: Chimee Eze.

Additional content available online at http://realsqlqueries.com.

ABOUT THE AUTHORS

Brian Cohen

Brian Cohen is Senior Data Analyst at Healthesystems. He earned his Bachelor of Arts in Economics from University of South Florida. Making the most of Spotify, Brian usually writes SQL alongside the music of Neil Young and The Grateful Dead. Feel free to contact Brian at cohenbrian@gmail.com with comments, ideas, or gentle criticism.

Many thanks to Brian's wife René for her encouragement throughout the process of creating the book. Brian also thanks Gordon Bennett, Steve Caron, and many other former colleagues at Bisk Education where, years ago, he launched Management Studio for the first time.

Neil Pepi

Neil learned a lot of what he knows today at Bisk Education, where he is currently Senior Database Marketing Analyst. Bisk created an environment that holds practical, on-the-job learning as a priority. He would be remiss if he didn't thank the owners of Bisk Education and all the talented people that work there.

Neil earned his Bachelor of Science in Accounting from the University of South Florida. He can be contacted at neilpepi1@gmail.com.

Neerja Mishra

Neerja Mishra is a SQL Developer currently working with Citibank in Tampa Florida. She graduated from University of Delhi, India with a Bachelor in Science and she earned her Master's in Engineering from South Dakota State University. Besides her work, she enjoys music, travelling, watching documentaries and reading. Neerja Mishra can be contacted at nes1711@hotmail.com.

TABLE OF CONTENTS

About the Authors iii

Introduction ix

    The Challenges ix
    The Solutions ix
    What's Needed ix
    Organization x

Exploring a New Database 1

Challenge Questions 3

    Challenge Question 1: Year over Year Comparisons 3
    Challenge Question 2: The 2/22 Promotion 4
    Challenge Question 3: Ten Million Dollar Benchmark 5
    Challenge Question 4: Upsell Tuesdays 6
    Challenge Question 5: Expired Credit Cards 7
    Challenge Question 6: Print Catalog 8
    Challenge Question 7: Special Offers 9
    Challenge Question 8: Similar Products 10
    Challenge Question 9: Product Combinations 11
    Challenge Question 10: Median Revenue 12
    Challenge Question 11: Needy Accountant 12
    Challenge Question 12: Product Inventory Updates 12
    Challenge Question 13: Vacation Hours 13
    Challenge Question 14: Purchasing 13
    Challenge Question 15: Interpretation Needed 14
    Challenge Question 16: Online/Offline 14
    Challenge Question 17: Long Time No Sale 15
    Challenge Question 18: Costs Vary 15
    Challenge Question 19: Thermoform Temperature 16
    Challenge Question 20: Toronto 16
    Challenge Question 21: Marketing Employees 17
    Challenge Question 22: Who Left That Review? 17
    Challenge Question 23: Label Mix-Up 18
    Challenge Question 24: Clearance Sale 18
    Challenge Question 25: Top Territories 19
    Challenge Question 26: Commission Percentages 19

Challenge Question 27: Work Orders 20
Challenge Question 28: Revenue Trended 20
Challenge Question 29: Separation 21
Challenge Question 30: Shift Coverage 21
Challenge Question 31: Labels 22
Challenge Question 32: Employment Survey 23
Challenge Question 33: Age Groups 24
Challenge Question 34: Revenue by State 24
Challenge Question 35: Two Free Bikes 25
Challenge Question 36: Volume Discounts 25
Challenge Question 37: Overpaying 26
Challenge Question 38: Margins 26
Challenge Question 39: Percent to Quota 27
Challenge Question 40: Revenue Ranges 28
Challenge Question 41: E-mail Mystery 29
Challenge Question 42: The Mentors 30
Challenge Question 43: Calendar of Work Days 31
Challenge Question 44: Annual Salary by Employee 31
Challenge Question 45: Annual Salaries by Department 32
Challenge Question 46: Holiday Bonus 32
Challenge Question 47: Company Picnic 33
Challenge Question 48: Sales Quota Changes 33
Challenge Question 49: Scrap Rate 34
Challenge Question 50: Reasons 34
Challenge Question 51: Excess Inventory 35
Challenge Question 52: Pay Rate Changes 35
Challenge Question 53: Sales Order Counts 36
Challenge Question 54: Loyal Customers 37
Challenge Question 55: Date Range Gaps 37

Hints for Challenge Questions 38

Hints for Challenge Question 1: Year over Year Comparisons 38
Hints for Challenge Question 2: The 2/22 Promotion 38
Hints for Challenge Question 3: Ten Million Dollar Benchmark 38
Hints for Challenge Question 4: Upsell Tuesdays 38
Hints for Challenge Question 5: Expired Credit Cards 39
Hints for Challenge Question 6: Print Catalog 39
Hints for Challenge Question 7: Special Offers 39
Hints for Challenge Question 8: Similar Products 39
Hints for Challenge Question 9: Product Combinations 40
Hints for Challenge Question 10: Median Revenue 40
Hints for Challenge Question 11: Needy Accountant 40
Hints for Challenge Question 12: Product Inventory Updates 40
Hints for Challenge Question 13: Vacation Hours 41

Hints for Challenge Question 14: Purchasing 41
Hints for Challenge Question 15: Interpretation Needed 41
Hints for Challenge Question 16: Online/Offline 41
Hints for Challenge Question 17: Long Time No Sale 41
Hints for Challenge Question 18: Costs Vary 41
Hints for Challenge Question 19: Thermoform Temperature 42
Hints for Challenge Question 20: Toronto 42
Hints for Challenge Question 21: Marketing Employees 42
Hints for Challenge Question 22: Who Left That Review? 42
Hints for Challenge Question 23: Label Mix-Up 42
Hints for Challenge Question 24: Clearance Sale 43
Hints for Challenge Question 25: Top Territories 43
Hints for Challenge Question 26: Commission Percentages 43
Hints for Challenge Question 27: Work Orders 43
Hints for Challenge Question 28: Revenue Trended 43
Hints for Challenge Question 29: Separation 43
Hints for Challenge Question 30: Shift Coverage 44
Hints for Challenge Question 31: Labels 44
Hints for Challenge Question 32: Employment Survey 44
Hints for Challenge Question 33: Age Groups 44
Hints for Challenge Question 34: Revenue by State 44
Hints for Challenge Question 35: Two Free Bikes 45
Hints for Challenge Question 36: Volume Discounts 45
Hints for Challenge Question 37: Overpaying 45
Hints for Challenge Question 38: Margins 45
Hints for Challenge Question 39: Percent to Quota 45
Hints for Challenge Question 40: Revenue Ranges 46
Hints for Challenge Question 41: E-mail Mystery 46
Hints for Challenge Question 42: The Mentors 46
Hints for Challenge Question 43: Calendar of Work Days 46
Hints for Challenge Question 44: Annual Salary by Employee 47
Hints for Challenge Question 45: Annual Salaries by Department 47
Hints for Challenge Question 46: Holiday Bonus 47
Hints for Challenge Question 47: Company Picnic 47
Hints for Challenge Question 48: Sales Quota Changes 48
Hints for Challenge Question 49: Scrap Rate 48
Hints for Challenge Question 50: Reasons 48
Hints for Challenge Question 51: Excess Inventory 48
Hints for Challenge Question 52: Pay Rate Changes 48
Hints for Challenge Question 53: Sales Order Counts 48
Hints for Challenge Question 54: Loyal Customers 48
Hints for Challenge Question 55: Date Range Gaps 49

Solutions to Challenge Questions **50**

Solution 1 to Challenge Question 1: Year over Year Comparisons 50
Solution 2 to Challenge Question 1: Year over Year Comparisons 51
Solution to Challenge Question 2: The 2/22 Promotion 52
Solution 1 to Challenge Question 3: Ten Million Dollar Benchmark 54
Solution 2 to Challenge Question 3: Ten Million Dollar Benchmark 55
Solution to Challenge Question 4: Upsell Tuesdays 55
Solution to Challenge Question 5: Expired Credit Cards 56
Solution to Challenge Question 6: Print Catalog 57
Solution 1 to Challenge Questions 7: Special Offers 57
Solution 2 to Challenge Questions 7: Special Offers 58
Solution 3 to Challenge Questions 7: Special Offers 58
Solution to Challenge Question 8: Similar Products 59
Solution to Challenge Question 9: Product Combinations 60
Solution 1 to Challenge Question 10: Median Revenue 62
Solution 2 to Challenge Question 10: Median Revenue 63
Solution to Challenge Question 11: Needy Accountant 63
Solution to Challenge Question 12: Product Inventory Updates 64
Solution to Challenge Question 13: Vacation Hours 64
Solution to Challenge Question 14: Purchasing 65
Solution to Challenge Question 15: Interpretation Needed 65
Solution to Challenge Question 16: Online/Offline 66
Solution to Challenge Question 17: Long Time No Sale 67
Solution to Challenge Question 18: Costs Vary 68
Solution to Challenge Question 19: Thermoform Temperature 69
Solution to Challenge Question 20: Toronto 70
Solution to Challenge Question 21: Marketing Employees 70
Solution to Challenge Question 22: Who Left That Review? 71
Solution to Challenge Question 23: Label Mix-Up 71
Solution to Challenge Question 24: Clearance Sale 72
Solution to Challenge Question 25: Top Territories 73
Solution to Challenge Question 26: Commission Percentages 73
Solution to Challenge Question 27: Work Orders 74
Solution to Challenge Question 28: Revenue Trended 75
Solution to Challenge Question 29: Separation 75
Solution to Challenge Question 30: Shift Coverage 76
Solution to Challenge Question 31: Labels 76
Solution to Challenge Question 32: Employment Survey 77
Solution to Challenge Question 33: Age Groups 78
Solution to Challenge Question 34: Revenue by State 79
Solution to Challenge Question 35: Two Free Bikes 79
Solution to Challenge Question 36: Volume Discounts 80
Solution to Challenge Question 37: Overpaying 81
Solution to Challenge Question 38: Margins 82
Solution to Challenge Question 39: Percent to Quota 83
Solution to Challenge Question 40: Revenue Ranges 84

Solution to Challenge Question 41: E-mail Mystery 85
Solution to Challenge Question 42: The Mentors 85
Solution to Challenge Question 43: Calendar of Work Days 86
Solution to Challenge Question 44: Annual Salaries by Employee 87
Solution to Challenge Question 45: Annual Salaries by Department 88
Solution 1 to Challenge Question 46: Holiday Bonus 89
Solution 2 to Challenge Question 46: Holiday Bonus 89
Solution 3 to Challenge Question 46: Holiday Bonus 90
Solution to Challenge Question 47: Company Picnic 90
Solution to Challenge Question 48: Sales Quota Changes 91
Solution to Challenge Question 49: Scrap Rate 91
Solution to Challenge Question 50: Reasons 92
Solution to Challenge Question 51: Excess Inventory 93
Solution 1 to Challenge Question 52: Pay Rate Changes 94
Solution 2 to Challenge Question 52: Pay Rate Changes 95
Solution 1 to Challenge Question 53: Sales Order Counts 95
Solution 2 to Challenge Question 53: Sales Order Counts 96
Solution to Challenge Question 54: Loyal Customers 96
Solution to Challenge Question 55: Date Range Gaps 97

Index 98

INTRODUCTION

We, the authors, are practical developers. While we are interested in conceptual learning, we think real problem solving is king. In textbooks, we skip to the practice queries. At work, we scour the internet for coding techniques to answer questions about our business. We're most excited by SQL queries that get the job done.

With more than 50 challenge questions, this book enables the practical developer. To make the material more relatable, we've designed the challenges with report writers and analysts in mind. And we've tailored all challenges to AdventureWorks2012, Microsoft's universally-accessible sample database, so that you can begin querying immediately.

The Challenges
The difficulty of the challenges throughout the book is mixed, so the material accommodates many backgrounds. Some questions are simple, while others call for strategic, multi-step solutions. We aimed to include a broad group of SQL users within our audience.

The Solutions
We believe independent reasoning is essential. Accordingly, solutions are provided but not necessarily dissected. We empower you to think through our code without interruption or noise.

Our solutions favor human logic and readability over performance. We worked through the problems in ways that were rational to us while carrying reasonable efficiency. Performance tuning is certainly worthy, but its craft falls outside the scope of this book.

There are many possible approaches to any given solution, so you're likely to discover alternate routes that feel more appropriate. Likewise, numerous coding styles exist, and our preferences may not line up with yours. We encourage you to rewrite the SQL as you see fit.

What's Needed
The book is best supported by SQL Server 2012 or higher with AdventureWorks2012. The Express version of SQL Server 2012 is free, so you should install the software if needed. AdventureWorks2012 is free as well.

The following links should assist you with downloads and installations:

SQL Server Downloads
https://goo.gl/u1R1vY

AdventureWorks2012 Download
https://goo.gl/LNfoiM

Organization

The book is divided into two parts. In Part I, we begin with a discussion about navigating relationships among unfamiliar tables. We've outlined ideas to help you prepare the right road map for the right problem-solving journey. Part I continues with lots of varied challenge questions for you try.

In Part II, you'll find hints, strategies, and solutions. We placed this material far away from the challenge questions by design. You won't accidentally bump into unwanted answers while you're working through questions. As mentioned earlier, we enable you to think without interruption.

We've prepared each solution as a distinct .sql file for download. Feel free to retrieve whichever files you like at http://realsqlqueries.com.

EXPLORING A NEW DATABASE

It is not uncommon for a report writer or analyst to be thrown into a new database with little to no guidance, let alone a data dictionary. For exactly these reasons, it can be beneficial to be able to investigate a database yourself before asking your coworkers unnecessary questions. Luckily, SQL Server has a lot of robust tools built-in for conducting such research.

For example, let's say you want to find a column somewhere in the database, but you're not sure what table it exists on. The code below can do exactly that; all you have to do is replace the database name and the column name you're searching for.

```sql
USE DatabaseName
GO

--DROP TABLE #data

SELECT
    TableView =   ISNULL (N2.Name, N3.Name)
    ,ObjectView=  CASE WHEN N2.Name IS NOT NULL THEN 'Table' ELSE 'View' END
    ,ColName =    N1.Name
INTO #data
FROM sys.columns N1
LEFT JOIN sys.tables N2 ON N1.object_id = N2.object_id
LEFT JOIN sys.views N3 ON N1.object_id = N3.object_id
WHERE N2.object_id IS NOT NULL
    OR N3.object_id IS NOT NULL
ORDER BY TableView

SELECT *
FROM #data
WHERE ColName LIKE '%ColumnName%'
```

Now, let's say you've found the table you want to use, but you're not entirely sure how it's structured. For example, how do you find out if a column is unique if there isn't a primary key constraint? The code below can show you any value for the field selected that has more than one row. If this query returns no results, the field you've chosen is unique.

```
SELECT ColumnName
FROM TableName
GROUP BY ColumnName
HAVING COUNT (*) > 1
```

If we augment that code slightly, we can now check for relationships. The following query is checking if any values exist for ColumnName1 that have multiple values in ColumnName2.

```
SELECT ColumnName1
FROM TableName
GROUP BY ColumnName1
HAVING COUNT (DISTINCT ColumnName2) > 1
```

If we then run the opposite, we can determine the relationship between these two columns.

```
SELECT ColumnName2
FROM TableName
GROUP BY ColumnName2
HAVING COUNT (DISTINCT ColumnName1) > 1
```

Based on the results, the table below can show you the relationship between ColumnName1 and ColumnName2.

		Second Query	
		Returns results	Does not return results
First Query	Returns results	many : many	1 : many
	Does not return results	many : 1	1 : 1

CHALLENGE QUESTIONS

Challenge Question 1: Year over Year Comparisons
Difficulty: Intermediate

An executive requests data concerning fiscal quarter sales by salesperson. She'd like to see comparisons from the fiscal quarters of 2008 to the same fiscal quarters of 2007.

For example, suppose sales for salesperson X totaled $1,000 during Fiscal Year 2008, Fiscal Quarter 2. If sales for salesperson X totaled $900 in Fiscal Year 2007, Fiscal Quarter 2, this reflects about 11.1% growth between the two periods for salesperson X.

Notes:

- For Adventure Works, the fiscal year spans July through June
- Tax and freight will not be considered with revenue
- Dates are based on OrderDate
- Disregard online orders

Your output should include the following columns, corresponding to all sales people:

- LastName
- SalesPersonID
- Fiscal year
- Fiscal quarter
- Fiscal quarter sales
- Sales during the same fiscal quarter of the previous fiscal year
- Change in revenue between the two periods
- Percent change in revenue between the two periods

Following the same example, your output for one row would appear as follows:

LastName	SalesPersonID	FY	FQ	FQSales	SalesSameFQLast	Change	%Change
X	1	2008	2	1000	900	100	11.1

Challenge Question 2: The 2/22 Promotion
Difficulty: Intermediate

A marketing manager devised the "2/22" promotion, in which orders subtotaling at least $2,000 ship for $0.22. The strategy assumes that freight losses will be offset by gains from higher value orders. According to the marketing manager, orders between $1,700 and $2,000 will likely boost to $2,000 as customers feel compelled to take advantage of bargain freight pricing.

You are asked to test the 2/22 promotion for hypothetical profitability based on the marketing manager's assumption about customer behavior. Examine orders shipped to California during fiscal year 2008 for net gains or losses under the promotion.

PART I
Create a table that includes the following columns:

- SalesOrderID
- Ship to state (California)
- OrderDate
- Historical order subtotal (prior to any changes as a result of the promotion)
- Historical freight (prior to any changes as a result of the promotion)
- Potential promotional effect. Indicate one of three hypothetical scenarios related to the order:
    - Increase order to $2,000 and pay $0.22 freight
    - No order change and pay $0.22 freight
    - No order change and pay historical freight
- Potential order gain
- Potential freight loss
- Potential promotional net gain/loss

Notes:

- For Adventure Works, the fiscal year spans July through June
- Tax should not be considered

PART II
Aggregate data from Part I by PotentialPromotionalEffect. Include the following:

- PotentialPromotionalEffect
- Potential order gains
- Potential freight losses
- Overall net gain/loss

Challenge Question 3: Ten Million Dollar Benchmark
Difficulty: Intermediate

Ten million dollars of revenue is a common benchmark for Adventure Works. For each fiscal year (2007 and 2008), find the first dates when the cumulative running revenue total hit $10 million.

Notes:

- For Adventure Works, the fiscal year spans July through June
- Do not consider tax and freight with revenue

Your output should include the following columns:

- Fiscal year (2007 or 2008)
- Order date in which $10 million was reached or exceeded
- Order number within the fiscal year in which $10 million was reached or exceeded. Note, this is a count of orders. For example, if the $10 million goal was reached on the 50th order, then the appropriate value to report is 50.
- Running total revenue in which $10 million was reached or exceeded

Example output:

FiscalYear	OrderDate	FYOrder#	RunningTotal
2007	7/10/2007	6	10,000,008
2008	7/29/2007	5	10,000,012

Challenge Question 4: Upsell Tuesdays
Difficulty: Beginner

Tuesday's are "upsell" days for sales people at Adventure Works. Management wants to compare sales from Tuesday to other days of the week to see if the initiative is working. Help monitor the upsell initiative by creating a query to calculate average revenue per order by day of week in 2008.

Include the following columns with your output:

- Day of week
- Revenue
- Orders
- Revenue per order

Notes:

- Dates based on OrderDate
- Tax and freight should not be considered
- Exclude online orders

Challenge Question 5: Expired Credit Cards
Difficulty: Intermediate

The Accounting department found instances where expired credit cards were used with sales orders. You are asked to examine all credit cards and report the extent of such activity.

PART I
Based on each CreditCardID, find the following:

- CreditCardType
- ExpirationDate
- Last order date
- Number of sales orders with order dates earlier than or equal to the card's expiration date
- Number of sales orders with order dates later than the card's expiration date

Note:
Adventure Works stores information about a credit card's expiration year and expiration month. Expiration dates pertain to the last day of a card's expiration month. For example, if the expiration year is 2007 and the expiration month is "4", the card's expiration date will be April 30, 2007.

PART II
Based on CreditCardType, summarize data returned from Part I. Your output should include the following columns:

- CreditCardType
- Number of sales orders with order dates earlier than or equal to the card's expiration date
- Number of sales orders with order dates later than the card's expiration date

Challenge Question 6: Print Catalog
Difficulty: Beginner

Adventure Works will feature one product for the cover of its print catalog. Help select a list of products for consideration.

Your list should contain products which meet all the following conditions:

- Finished goods (not products utilized to make other products)
- List price at least $1,500
- At least 150 in inventory
- Currently available for sale

Your output should contain the following columns:

- ProductID
- ProductName
- Color
- ListPrice
- Inventory quantity

Challenge Question 7: Special Offers
Difficulty: Beginner

A new manager believes that Special Offers have been underutilized.

During a Special Offer meeting, you are asked to create a report about Special Offers NOT assigned to products.

Once Special Offers not assigned to products have been identified, report the following information:

- SpecialOfferID
- Special Offer Description
- Special Offer End Date

All results must reflect Special Offers that have not yet ended, with discounts greater than 0%.
To evaluate ending dates, assume today is January 1, 2008.

Challenge Question 8: Similar Products
Difficulty: Intermediate

Create a report to aid salespeople. The report will display information about similar, less expensive products to suggest.

Similar products:

- Share the same subcategory as the base product. For example, if the base product is classified as a Mountain Bike, the similar product should be a Mountain Bike as well.
- Share the same size as the base product.
- Share the same style as the base product.
- Are less expensive, Based on List Price, than the base product.

Suppose today is January 1, 2014. All products listed within the report must be:

- Available for sale
- Finished Goods (not products utilized to make other products)

If more than one similar product meets all conditions, report the one closest in price to the Base product.

Your report should contain the following columns:

Base Product ID

- Base Product Name
- Base Product Price
- Similar Product Price
- Similar Product Name
- Similar Product ID

Example Output:

Base_Prod_ID	Base_Prod_Name	Base_Prod_Price	Similar_Prod_Price	Similar_Prod_Name	Similar_Product_ID
780	Mountain-200 Silver, 42	2319.99	2294.99	Mountain-200 Black, 42	783

Challenge Question 9: Product Combinations
Difficulty: Advanced

The executive management team wants to analyze the buying behavior of customers.

PART I
Provide the following calculations:

- Percentage of sales orders containing at least one bike and at least one accessory item
- Percentage of sales orders containing at least one bike and at least two different clothing products

PART II
Count sales orders by product type. For example, if 500 sales orders included the product types Bikes and Clothing, with no accessories and components purchased, that output row would appear as follows:

Bikes	Accessories	Clothing	Components	Orders
1	0	1	0	500

PART III
Count customers by product line. For example, if 100 customers purchased products from product lines M and T, but not S and R, that output row would appear as follows:

M	S	T	R	Customers
1	0	1	0	100

Challenge Question 10: Median Revenue
Difficulty: Intermediate

An analyst notified the Vice President of Sales that averages can be skewed by outliers. In response, he asks to see median revenue in addition to average revenue. He also asks you to add minimum and maximum revenue to your report.

Write a query of sales by year that includes the following columns:

- Order year
- Minimum sale
- Maximum sale
- Average sale
- Median sale

Notes:

- Years based on OrderDate
- Tax and freight should not be considered with revenue

Challenge Question 11: Needy Accountant
Difficulty: Beginner

An accountant needs to add assumptions about sales tax rates to his Excel worksheet. He asks you to provide one sales tax rate, conservatively, for each of the countries in which tax rates are known.

To fulfill his request, report the maximum sales tax rate of each country.

Challenge Question 12: Product Inventory Updates
Difficulty: Advanced

You are asked to provide frequent updates about the Adventure Works product inventory. Create a View that includes the following:

- Number of distinct products by LocationID
- Quantity of products by LocationID
- A rollup with total number of distinct products throughout all LocationIDs
- A rollup with total quantity of products throughout all LocationIDs

Challenge Question 13: Vacation Hours
Difficulty: Intermediate

Human Resources is reevaluating a policy about maximum allowable vacation rollover hours. You are asked to help by identifying the employee or group of employees with the greatest number of vacation hours. Since many Human Resources files are indexed by NationalIDNumber, please include the last four digits with your output.

In all, your output should contain the following information:

- Last four digits of NationalIDNumber
- FirstName
- LastName
- JobTitle
- Number of vacation hours

Challenge Question 14: Purchasing
Difficulty: Intermediate

For each product ordered by the Purchasing Department in 2007, indicate the quantity ordered by order date. In all, include the following columns with your output:

- ProductID
- Product name
- OrderDate
- Quantity ordered

Arrange data in descending order by quantity ordered.

Challenge Question 15: Interpretation Needed
Difficulty: Intermediate

The Adventure Works Marketing department utilizes contractors to review foreign language product descriptions. To help the contractors, you are asked to prepare a list of all product descriptions written in languages other than English.

Your output should contain the following columns:

- ProductModelID
- Name of product model
- Product description
- Language

Challenge Question 16: Online/Offline
Difficulty: Beginner

Create a summary table that shows, by territory, the percentage of orders placed online in comparison to orders not placed online.

Your output should include the following columns:

- TerritoryID
- Total orders
- Percentage of orders placed online
- Percentage of orders not placed online

To make the table easier to read, display percentages with a percent sign without decimals. For example, ninety five percent will be displayed as 95%.

Challenge Question 17: Long Time No Sale
Difficulty: Intermediate

The sales department will visit stores without recent sales orders. Suppose today's date is October 7, 2008. Create a report that identifies stores in which the last order date was at least 12 months ago.

Your output should include the following columns:

- BusinessEntityID
- CustomerID
- StoreID
- StoreName
- Last order date
- Number of months since last order

Challenge Question 18: Costs Vary
Difficulty: Intermediate

A team was formed with the goal of reducing product costs. Help the team kick off their first meeting by compiling baseline data about historical product cost variability.

Query the data by ProductID. Your output should include the following:

- ProductID
- ProductName
- SubCategory
- Minimum historical cost
- Maximum historical cost
- Historical cost variability (maximum historical cost minus minimum historical cost)
- Ranking of all historical cost variabilities (rank of "1" reflects the product ID exhibiting the greatest historical cost variability)

Challenge Question 19: Thermoform Temperature
Difficulty: Intermediate

You are asked to report the most common reasons why products were scrapped through the manufacturing process. Create a query by ProductID that includes the following:

- ProductID
- ProductName
- Number of work orders affected
- Most common scrap reason

For example, suppose "Thermoform temperature too high" was the most common reason why ProductID 398 was scrapped. If the product was scrapped 100 times as a result of this reason, your row about the product would appear as follows:

ProductID	ProductName	WorkOrderCount	ScrapReason
398	Handlebar Tube	100	Thermoform temperature too high

Challenge Question 20: Toronto
Difficulty: Intermediate

Provide address data about stores with main offices located in Toronto.

Your output should include the following columns:

- Store name
- AddressLine1
- AddressLine2
- City
- StateProvince
- PostalCode

Challenge Question 21: Marketing Employees
Difficulty: Intermediate

An administrator from Human Resources asks you for a list of employees who are currently in the Marketing department and were hired prior to 2002 or later than 2004.

Your output should include the following columns:

- FirstName
- LastName
- JobTitle
- BirthDate
- MaritalStatus
- HireDate

Challenge Question 22: Who Left That Review?
Difficulty: Intermediate

The executives want to know if it's possible to link people who have made product reviews with customer data. The end goal is to link sales information to product reviews.

As a first step, try looking up BusinessEntityID of reviewers based on e-mail addresses. If known, BusinessEntityIDs can point to sales orders through CustomerIDs.

Your output should include the following columns:

- ProductReviewID
- Product ID
- Product name
- ReviewerName
- Rating
- Reviewer's email address
- Reviewer's BusinessEntityID (if known)

Challenge Question 23: Label Mix-Up
Difficulty: Intermediate

Some clothing items were mislabeled, and management will inform customers. You are asked to help by compiling a list of affected customers with phone numbers. The issue pertains to all orders for shorts placed online after July 7, 2008.

Your list should contain the following columns:

- SalesOrderID
- OrderDate
- ProductName
- Customer's first name
- Customer's last name
- Customer's phone number

Challenge Question 24: Clearance Sale
Difficulty: Intermediate

The Marketing department will prepare a mass e-mail to notify individual retail customers about a clearance sale. You are asked to report the depth of e-mail addresses within the company's databases.

According the requestor, e-mail address counts should be based on e-mail preferences. E-mail preferences are recorded in the Person.Person table within the column EmailPromotion.

Utilize the following e-mail preference conversions as part of your output:

- The value "0" indicates "Contact does not wish to receive e-mail promotions"
- The value "1" indicates "Contact does wish to receive e-mail promotions from AdventureWorks"
- The value "2" indicates "Contact does wish to receive e-mail promotions from AdventureWorks and selected partners"

Example output:

Email Preference	Count
Contact does not with to receive e-mail promotions	500
Contact does wish to receive e-mail promotions from AdventureWorks	400
Contact does wish to receive e-mail promotions from AdventureWorks and selected partners	300

Challenge Question 25: Top Territories
Difficulty: Intermediate

In terms of revenue, which two sales territories were top performers during fiscal years 2006 and 2007?

Notes:

- For AdventureWorks, the fiscal year spans July through June
- Tax and freight will not be considered with revenue

Your output should include the following columns:

- Fiscal year
- Territory name
- Revenue
- Territory rank

Challenge Question 26: Commission Percentages
Difficulty: Beginner

Rank commission percentages by sales person.

Notes:

- A rank of "1" should relate to the sales person with the greatest commission percentage
- If commission percentages are equal among sales people, rank by Bonus in descending order

Your solution should include the following columns:

- BusinessEntityID
- Commission percent
- Bonus
- Rank

Challenge Question 27: Work Orders
Difficulty: Beginner

PART I
The Production department asks you to report the number of work orders by ProductID. Order your results from the greatest number of work orders to the least.

PART II
Report the number of work orders by product name. Order your results from the greatest number of work orders to the least.

Challenge Question 28: Revenue Trended
Difficulty: Intermediate

PART I
Suppose today's date is May 24, 2008. Using only revenue information from May 1 through May 23, estimate revenue for the whole month of May.

Notes:

- Dates are based on OrderDate
- Tax and freight will not be considered with revenue

Your output should include the following columns:

- Number of days in month so far
- Total revenue in month so far
- Revenue per day for the month so far
- Monthly revenue trended for all of May

PART II
For the sake of comparison, pull the actual revenue information.

Your output should include the following columns:

- Actual revenue per day
- Actual revenue

Challenge Question 29: Separation
Difficulty: Intermediate

The HumanResources.Employee table includes the column LoginID in which user names and domains are combined.

In your query, separate the names from the domains. Your output should include the following:

- BusinessEntityID
- LoginID (for example, adventure-works\ken0)
- Domain (for example, adventure-works)
- Username (for example, ken0)

Challenge Question 30: Shift Coverage
Difficulty: Intermediate

Management will review the current distribution of labor by shift within the Production department.

Create a report that includes the following:

- Department name (Production)
- Shift name
- Number of employees

Challenge Question 31: Labels
Difficulty: Beginner

Labels representing product sizes will be applied to the boxes and packages of some products. The variety of labels include "S" (size "Small"), "M" (size "Medium"), "L" (size "Large"), and "XL" (size "Extra Large").

PART I

Write a query to determine if the variety of labels is sufficient to cover all alpha-sized products. For example, since "2XL" labels do not exist, no label could be applied to a "2XL" product. If a "2XL" product existed, the variety of labels would be insufficient.

PART II

Suppose 1,000 labels are available in each size. Calculate the number of additional labels needed to cover all the relevant products in the inventory.

By size, create a table that includes the following columns:

- Size
- Current quantity
- Additional labels needed

Challenge Question 32: Employment Survey
Difficulty: Intermediate

Adventure Works will participate in a third-party employment survey among bicycle manufacturers. The Human Resources department asks you to help prepare data to submit.

PART I
Provide the following:

- Total number of employees throughout the company
- Percentage of employees who are Male
- Percentage of employees who are Female
- Average number of months of employment. Pretend today is January 1, 2008.

Sample output:

Employees	%Male	%Female	AvgMonthsEmployed
100	50.00	50.00	10

PART II
Divide employee data into quartiles based on average number of months of employment. By quartile, provide the following:

- Total number of employees throughout the company
- Percentage of employees who are Male
- Percentage of employees who are Female
- Average number of months employed. Pretend today is January 1, 2008.

Sample output:

Quartile	Employees	%Male	%Female	AvgMonthsEmployed
1	25	50.00	50.00	10
2	25	50.00	50.00	10

Challenge Question 33: Age Groups
Difficulty: Intermediate

In the previous question, you provided data for a third-party employment survey among bicycle manufacturers. More information is needed.

Create a query summarizing pay rates and age groups by job title. Assume today is January 1, 2008. Your output should be structured with the following columns:

- JobTitle
- Age group, in years, categorized as follows:
    - < 18
    - 18 – 35
    - 36 – 50
    - 51 – 60
    - 61 +
- Pay rate
- Number of employees

As an example, if 10 Production Assistants were 39 years old on January 1, 2008, and their pay rate was 23.65, the corresponding output row would appear as follows:

JobTitle	AgeGroup	Rate	Employees
Production Assistant	36 – 50	23.65	10

Challenge Question 34: Revenue by State
Difficulty: Beginner

Report revenue by state in 2006. Order the data from states with the greatest revenue to states with the least revenue.

Notes:

- Dates based on OrderDate
- Revenue includes tax and freight
- States based on shipping address

Challenge Question 35: Two Free Bikes
Difficulty: Intermediate

Two employees are given free bicycles at the start of each quarterly meeting. The employees are chosen at random, with eligibility limited to the least senior positions.

Create a view to generate employee names. The view should include the following columns:

- FirstName
- LastName
- JobTitle

Challenge Question 36: Volume Discounts
Difficulty: Intermediate

You are asked to report data about volume discounts.

PART I
Create a query about sales orders that utilized volume discounts.

Your output should include the following columns:

- SalesOrderID
- OrderDate
- Total volume discount (the sum of volume discounts applied to the order)

PART II
Summarize data from Part I by order year.

Include the following:

- Order year
- Total volume discount

Challenge Question 37: Overpaying
Difficulty: Intermediate

Some products are purchased from multiple vendors. Concerned about overpaying for products, the executive team asks to see price comparisons among vendors.

Using the Purchasing.ProductVendor table exclusively, determine if products are purchased at significantly lower prices from one vendor to another. By ProductID, create a query to return the following information:

- ProductID
- Most expensive price
- Second most expensive price
- Percent difference from most expensive price to second most expensive (expressed as a two-digit decimal. For example, a 93% price difference will be displayed as 0.93).

Challenge Question 38: Margins
Difficulty: Intermediate

Create a query calculating the profit margins of bike models.

Notes:

- Profit margin is based on the percent difference between ListPrice and StandardCost
- Only consider bike models currently sold

Your output should contain the following columns, with models exhibiting the greatest profit margins listed first.

- ProductModelID
- Product name
- Profit margin (expressed as a two-digit decimal. For example, a 93% profit margin will be displayed as 0.93)

Challenge Question 39: Percent to Quota
Difficulty: Intermediate

Each sales person is subject to a quarterly quota stated within the Sales.SalesPersonQuotaHistory table. The QuotaDate column represents the first date of the quota quarter.

PART I

Build a table to show the quota, actual sales, and percent to quota for each quarter and sales person. Store your data in a temporary table to be utilized in Part II.

Note: Do not include tax and freight with revenue.

Your results should contain the following columns:

- BusinessEntityID
- Quota date
- Sales quota
- Actual sales
- Percent to quota

Sort data by BusinessEntityID followed by quota date.

PART II

Summarize results from Part I by sales person, by year.

Include the following:

- Business Entity ID
- Quota year
- Total quota
- Total sales
- Total percent to quota
- Average quarterly percent to quota

Sort output by Business Entity ID followed by Quota year.

Challenge Question 40: Revenue Ranges
Difficulty: Beginner

Based on sales data from 2005, calculate the number of sales orders within each of the following revenue ranges:

1. $0 - $100
2. $100 - $500
3. $500 - $1,000
4. $1,000 - $2,500
5. $2,500 - $5,000
6. $5,000 - $10,000
7. $10,000 - $50,000
8. $50,000 - $100,000
9. > $100,000

Notes:

- Revenue includes tax and freight
- Dates based on OrderDate

Create a SortID to sort your results in the sequence presented above. Example output:

SortID	SalesAmountCategory	Orders
1	$0 - $100	10
2	$100 - $500	10
3	$500 - $1,000	10
4	$1,000 - $2,500	10
5	$2,500 - $5,000	10
6	$5,000 - $10,000	10
7	$10,000 - $50,000	10
8	$50,000 - $100,000	10
9	> $100,000	10

Challenge Question 41: E-mail Mystery
Difficulty: Intermediate

A sales person was unable to locate a returning customer's account by e-mail address. Frustrated, he pulled up the account by the customer's last name. With the account information on his screen, he realized why his customer's e-mail address was not found. The customer's e-mail address appeared as an "adventure-works.com" address, rather than "gmail.com."

Examine the prevalence of adventure-works.com e-mail addresses throughout the company's database. Create a query by PersonType, with the following output:

- PersonType
- Number of e-mail addresses containing the adventure-works.com domain
- Number of e-mail addresses not containing the adventure-works.com domain
- Total number of e-mail addresses

Display your results by the greatest number of e-mail addresses to the fewest number of e-mail addresses.

Challenge Question 42: The Mentors
Difficulty: Intermediate

The Vice President of Sales wants the five most successful sales people to mentor the five least successful sales people. Create a list of sales people to match with one another.

Notes:

- Success is measured by 2008 revenue.
- Dates are based on OrderDate.
- Do not consider tax and freight with revenue.
- Ignore orders with no SalesPersonID.

Your output should contain the following columns:

- SalesPersonID of the successful sales person
- Revenue of the successful sales person
- SalesPersonID of the unsuccessful sales person
- Revenue of the successful sales person

For example, suppose the sales person with SalesPersonID 10 was the most successful sales person and her revenue was $1,000. If the sales person with SalesPersonID 20 was the least successful sales person and her revenue was $200, then the first row of your five-row output would appear as follows:

SuccessSalesPersonID	SuccessRevenue	UnsuccessSalesPersonID	UnsuccessRevenue
10	$1,000	20	$200

Challenge Question 43: Calendar of Work Days
Difficulty: Advanced

Calculate the number of work days in each year, without consideration for holidays, to help forecast energy costs. Use this exercise as an opportunity to create a comprehensive calendar of work days present in each year from January 1, 1990 to January 1, 2015 to be used for future purposes.

Save your calendar of work days as a table. Your table should contain the following columns:

- DateID (unique identifier)
- Date (for example, 1990-01-20 00:00:00.000)
- TextMonth (for example, January 1990)
- DateMonth (for example, 1990-01-01 00:00:00.000)
- DayOfWeek (for example, Monday)
- IsBusinessDay (0 or 1)

Based on the table you created, summarize the number of working days per year with the following columns:

- Year
- BusinessDays

Challenge Question 44: Annual Salary by Employee
Difficulty: Advanced

Create a query to show annual salary by employee from 2005 to 2008.

Assumptions:

- Today's date is January 1, 2009
- The Rate column within HumanResources.EmployeePayHistory represents hourly pay rates
- Each employee works eight hours per day, Monday through Friday

Notes:

- Holidays should not be considered
- You may utilize the calendar of work days created from Challenge Question 43.
- It would be helpful to utilize temporary tables; the next challenge question will incorporate information from this exercise

Challenge Question 45: Annual Salaries by Department
Difficulty: Advanced

The Vice President of Human Resources reviewed your report about annual salaries from Challenge Question 44. He liked your work and he asked to see data from an additional perspective.

Write a query about annual salaries by department from 2008. Your output should include the following columns:

- DepartmentID
- Minimum salary
- Average salary
- Maximum salary

Challenge Question 46: Holiday Bonus
Difficulty: Beginner

Human Resources will issue holiday bonuses to salaried employees. The bonus amount will equal current pay rate multiplied by 50. For example, an employee earning $10 per hour will receive a holiday bonus of $500.

Calculate holiday bonuses. Your output should include the following columns:

- BusinessEntityID
- FirstName
- LastName
- JobTitle
- Bonus

Challenge Question 47: Company Picnic
Difficulty: Intermediate

Name tags will be printed for a company picnic. You are asked to help prepare a list of employee names.

Create a query in which first names, last names, and suffixes are consolidated into one value, with a comma and a space separating the last name from the suffix. For example, if FirstName = David, LastName = Baez, and Suffix = Jr, the name would be consolidated as David Baez, Jr. If Suffix is NULL, the name appears as David Baez.

In all, your output should contain the following columns:

- BusinessEntityID
- Full name
- Department

Display the list alphabetically by department followed by full name.

Challenge Question 48: Sales Quota Changes
Difficulty: Intermediate

Management will review sales quota changes from 2006 through 2007. Create a report, by sales person, that includes the following information:

- BusinessEntityID
- LastName
- Sales quota from the start of 2006 (first quarter)
- Sales quota from the end of 2007 (last quarter)
- Percent change in sales quotas

For sound comparisons, do not include information about sales people who were not assigned sales quotas during the start of 2007 or the end of 2007.

Challenge Question 49: Scrap Rate
Difficulty: Intermediate

The Production department is concerned about work orders in which scrap rates exceed 3%. Scrap rate equals scrapped quantity divided by order quantity.

Create a view that displays, by most recent due dates, the top 10% of work orders in which the scrap rate was greater than 3%, ordered by most recent due date.

Your view should contain the following:

- WorkOrderID
- DueDate
- ProductName
- Scrap reason
- Scrapped quantity
- Order quantity
- Percent scrapped

Example output:

WorkOrderID	DueDate	ProdName	ScrappedQty	OrderQty	PercScrapped
10000	2008-01-01	Blade	10	20	50.00

Challenge Question 50: Reasons
Difficulty: Intermediate

Adventure Works collects data on some customer's reasons for purchasing (seen on Sales.SalesOrderHeaderSalesReason). Sometimes, customers cite one reason, like "Price," for ordering a product. Other times, customers cite multiple reasons, like "Price" and "Quality."

Create a query about sales order reasons. When a sales order has only one reason, categorize as "Exclusive Reason." When a sales order has more than one reason, categorize as "Contributing Reason." Then, create a summary count of sales orders by reason name and your newly created ReasonInfluence column (Exclusive Reason or Contributing Reason).

Based on the directions stated above, your output will contain the following columns:

- ReasonName
- ReasonInfluence (Exclusive Reason or Contributing Reason)
- SalesOrderCount

Challenge Question 51: Excess Inventory
Difficulty: Intermediate

Occasionally, Adventure Works has excess inventory on some of its products. To sell these overstocked products quickly, the company creates special discounts.

PART I
To help choose the discount percentage to be applied, create a query about historical excess inventory discounts. Pull a list of the previous excess inventory discounts Adventure Works has created.

Your output should contain the following columns:

- SpecialOfferID
- Discount type (Excess Inventory)
- Discount description
- Discount category (Customer or Reseller)
- Discount start date
- Discount end date
- Discount percentage

PART II
Add an additional column to the output from Part I. List the number of sales orders in which the discount was utilized.

Challenge Question 52: Pay Rate Changes
Difficulty: Intermediate

Human Resources will review pay increases. For each employee, report the latest pay rate and the pay rate prior to the latest rate.

Your output should include the following columns:

- BusinessEntityID
- Previous rate (Pay rate prior to the latest rate)
- Latest pay rate
- Percent change from previous rate to latest pay rate. Express the percent increase with two digits followed by a percent sign. For example, 10.01%

Challenge Question 53: Sales Order Counts

Difficulty: Intermediate

Create a report that lists order counts by salesperson by fiscal year.

For ease of readability, display your results as a grid. Example output:

LastName	FY2006	FY2007	FY2008
Ito	10	20	25
Jiang	12	13	15
Reiter	125	135	145
Vargas	3	5	6

The example reports 10 sales orders related to Ito within Fiscal Year 2006.

Notes:

- For Adventure Works, the fiscal year spans July through June
- Limit scope of data to fiscal Years 2006, 2007, and 2008.
- Dates are based on OrderDate
- Disregard online orders

Challenge Question 54: Loyal Customers
Difficulty: Intermediate

PART I
Provide a count of "loyal customers" in contrast to total customers. Customers are considered loyal when at least 10 orders are placed through a distinct sales person.

Your output should contain two columns:

- Count of loyal customers
- Count of all customers

Do not include sales in which the sales person is unknown.

PART II
Adapt your query from Part I to perform a check of reasonableness on your results. Display information about all sales orders relating to one, random loyal customer.

Challenge Question 55: Date Range Gaps
Difficulty: Intermediate

A pricing report returns unreasonable results. As a troubleshooting step, check the integrity of date ranges on Production.ProductListPriceHistory.

Each Product ID should correspond to Start Dates and End Dates with no gaps.

Example date ranges corresponding to one ProductID:

NO DATE GAPS

ProductID	StartDate	EndDate
999	2001-01-01	2001-12-31
999	2002-01-01	2002-12-31

DATE GAPS

ProductID	StartDate	EndDate
999	2001-01-01	2001-12-31
999	2002-01-15	2002-12-31

Your output should list any ProductID corresponding to any date gaps.

HINTS FOR CHALLENGE QUESTIONS

Hints for Challenge Question 1: Year over Year Comparisons

Key Table: Sales.SalesOrderHeader
Key Table: Person.Person

Strategy Step 1:

- Organize sales by salesperson, fiscal year, and fiscal quarter
- Exclude online orders
- Store results in temp table

Strategy Step 2:

- Find sales of the same quarter of the previous fiscal year by joining to the temp table

Hints for Challenge Question 2: The 2/22 Promotion

Key Table: Sales.SalesOrderHeader
Key Table: Person.BusinessEntityAddress
Key Table: Person.Address
Key Table: Person.StateProvince

Hints for Challenge Question 3: Ten Million Dollar Benchmark

Key Table: Sales.SalesOrderHeader
Key Column: OrderDate
Key Column: SubTotal

Hints for Challenge Question 4: Upsell Tuesdays

Key Table: Sales.SalesOrderHeader
Key Column: OnlineOrderFlag
Key Function: DATENAME

Hints for Challenge Question 5: Expired Credit Cards

Key Table: Sales.CreditCard
Key Function: EOMONTH
Key Function: DATEFROMPARTS
Key Table: Sales.SalesOrderHeader

Hints for Challenge Question 6: Print Catalog

Key Table: Production.Product
Key Column: SellEndDate
Key Column: FinishedGoodsFlag
Key Table: Production.ProductInventory

Hints for Challenge Question 7: Special Offers

Key Table: Sales.SpecialOffer
Key Table: Sales.SpecialOfferProduct

Hints for Challenge Question 8: Similar Products

Key Table: Production.Product
Key Table: Production.ProductSubcategory
Key Technique: Self-Join

Hints for Challenge Question 9: Product Combinations

Strategy: Build a temporary table with information about all sales orders. The table will be utilized throughout all parts of the solution. It should include at least the following columns:

- CustomerID
- SalesOrderID
- ProductType
- ProductLine
- ProductID

Key Table: Sales.SalesOrderHeader
Key Table: Sales.SalesOrderDetail
Key Table: Production.Product
Key Table: Production.ProductSubcategory
Key Table: Production.ProductCategory
Key Function: PIVOT

Hints for Challenge Question 10: Median Revenue

Key Table: Sales.SalesOrderHeader

Strategy:

- Create a row number for every order within each year
- Determine the maximum number of orders for each year
- Find the order with row number equal to half of the maximum number of orders

Key Function: PERCENTILE_DISC

Hints for Challenge Question 11: Needy Accountant

Key Table: Sales.SalesTaxRate
Key Table: Person.StateProvince
Key Table: Person.CountryRegion

Hints for Challenge Question 12: Product Inventory Updates

Key Table: Production.ProductInventory
Key Function: GROUPING
Key Operator: ROLLUP

Hints for Challenge Question 13: Vacation Hours

Key Table: HumanResources.Employee
Key Function: RIGHT

Hints for Challenge Question 14: Purchasing

Key Table: Purchasing.PurchaseOrderDetail
Key Table: Production.Product
Key Table: Purchasing.PurchaseOrderHeader

Hints for Challenge Question 15: Interpretation Needed

Key Table: Production.ProductDescription
Key Table: Production.ProductModelProductDescriptionCulture
Key Table: Production.ProductModel
Key Table: Production.Culture

Hints for Challenge Question 16: Online/Offline

Key Table: Sales.SalesOrderHeader
Key Column: OnlineOrderFlag
Key Function: CONVERT
Key Function: ROUND

Hints for Challenge Question 17: Long Time No Sale

Key Table: Sales.SalesOrderHeader
Key Table: Sales.Customer
Key Table: Sales.Store
Key Function: DATEDIFF

Hints for Challenge Question 18: Costs Vary

Key Table: Production.ProductCostHistory
Key Table: Production.Product
Key Table: Production.ProductSubcategory
Key Function: DENSE_RANK

Hints for Challenge Question 19: Thermoform Temperature

Key Table: Production.WorkOrder
Key Table: Production.Product
Key Table: Production.ScrapReason

Hints for Challenge Question 20: Toronto

Key Table: Person.BusinessEntityAddress
Key Table: Person.Address
Key Table: Person.AddressType
Key Table: Sales.Store

Hints for Challenge Question 21: Marketing Employees

Key Table: HumanResources.EmployeeDepartmentHistory
Key Column: EndDate (NULL indicates the current department)
Key Table: HumanResources.Department
Key Table: Person.Person
Key Table: HumanResources.Employee

Hints for Challenge Question 22: Who Left That Review?

Key Table: Production.ProductReview
Key Table: Production.Product
Key Table: Person.EmailAddress

Hints for Challenge Question 23: Label Mix-Up

Key Table: Sales.SalesOrderDetail
Key Table: Production.Product
Key Table: Sales.SalesOrderHeader
Key Table: Sales.Customer
Key Table: Person.Person
Key Table: Person.PersonPhone

Hints for Challenge Question 24: Clearance Sale

Key Table: Person.EmailAddress
Key Table: Person.Person
Key Column: PersonType
Key Value: IN (to locate individual retail customers)

Hints for Challenge Question 25: Top Territories

Key Table: Sales.SalesOrderHeader
Key Table: Sales.SalesTerritory
Key Function: DENSE_RANK

Hints for Challenge Question 26: Commission Percentages

Key Table: Sales.SalesPerson
Key Function: DENSE_RANK

Hints for Challenge Question 27: Work Orders

Key Table: Production.WorkOrder

Hints for Challenge Question 28: Revenue Trended

Key Table: Sales.SalesOrderHeader
Key Column: Subtotal
Key Function: EOMONTH

Hints for Challenge Question 29: Separation

Key Table: HumanResources.Employee
Key Function: LEFT
Key Function: CHARINDEX
Key Function: RIGHT
Key Function: LEN

Hints for Challenge Question 30: Shift Coverage

Key Table: HumanResources.EmployeeDepartmentHistory
Key Column: EndDate
Key Table: HumanResources.Department
Key Table: HumanResources.Shift

Hints for Challenge Question 31: Labels

PART I
Key Table: Production.Product
Key Function: ISNUMERIC

PART II
Key Table: Production.Product
Key Table: Production.ProductInventory

Hints for Challenge Question 32: Employment Survey

Key Table: HumanResources.Employee
Key Function: DATEDIFF
Key Function: NTILE

Hints for Challenge Question 33: Age Groups

Key Table: HumanResources.Employee
Key Function: DATEDIFF
Key Table: HumanResources.EmployeePayHistory

Hints for Challenge Question 34: Revenue by State

Key Table: Sales.SalesOrderHeader
Key Table: Person.Address
Key Table: Person.StateProvince

Hints for Challenge Question 35: Two Free Bikes

Key Table: HumanResources.Employee.

Key Column: OrganizationalLevel. Interpret the values of OrganizationalLevel appropriately by examining the values of various senior-level job titles.

Key Table: Person.Person

Hints for Challenge Question 36: Volume Discounts

Key Table: Sales.SalesOrderDetail
Key Table: Sales.SpecialOffer
Key Column: Type
Key Table: Sales.SalesOrderHeader

Hints for Challenge Question 37: Overpaying

Key Table: Purchasing.ProductVendor
Key Column: LastReceiptCost

Hints for Challenge Question 38: Margins

Key Table: Production.Product
Key Column: SellEndDate
Key Table: Production.ProductSubcategory
Key Table: Production.ProductCategory
Key Table: Production.ProductModel

Hints for Challenge Question 39: Percent to Quota

Key Table: Sales.SalesPersonQuotaHistory
Key Column: QuotaDate
Key Table: Sales.SalesOrderHeader

Key Consideration: Search for sales throughout the entire quarter. Since Quota Date represents the start of each quarter, the function DATEADD can be used to extend the date range.

Hints for Challenge Question 40: Revenue Ranges

Key Table: Sales.SalesOrderHeader
Key Column: TotalDue
Key Expression: CASE

Hints for Challenge Question 41: E-mail Mystery

Key Table: Person.EmailAddress
Key Table: Person.Person

Hints for Challenge Question 42: The Mentors

Key Table: Sales.SalesOrderHeader
Key Column: SalesPersonID
Key Column: Subtotal
Key Function: ROW_NUMBER

Hints for Challenge Question 43: Calendar of Work Days

Strategy to create the table about work days per year:

- Create a shell table with the necessary columns
- Create a loop that runs for the same amount of times as rows needed in the table
- Update table with details about each day

Key Functions:

- DATENAME
- DATEADD

Hints for Challenge Question 44: Annual Salary by Employee

As shown below, some BusinessEntityID's within the HumanResources.EmployeePayHistory table appear on multiple rows:

```
SELECT BusinessEntityID
FROM HumanResources.EmployeePayHistory
GROUP BY BusinessEntityID
HAVING COUNT (*) > 1
```

Each row may represent a pay rate change for employees with multiple pay rates over time.

Strategy:

- Identify the start date, end date, and the number of business days corresponding to each employee's range of dates for each pay rate.
- To count business days, utilize the calendar table you created through the previous challenge.

Hints for Challenge Question 45: Annual Salaries by Department

- You must account for the possibility that an employee can switch departments
- Key Table: HumanResources.EmployeeDepartmentHistory
- Utilize the calendar of work days from previous challenge to find data about employee pay

Hints for Challenge Question 46: Holiday Bonus

Key Table: HumanResources.Employee
Key Column: SalariedFlag
Key Table: HumanResources.EmployeePayHistory
Key Table: Person.Person

Hints for Challenge Question 47: Company Picnic

Key Table: Person.Person
Key Column: PersonType
Key Values: SP (Sales person), EM (non-sales employee)
Key Table: HumanResources.EmployeeDepartmentHistory
Key Table: HumanResources.Department

Hints for Challenge Question 48: Sales Quota Changes

Key Table: Sales.SalesQuotaPersonHistory
Key Table: Person.Person

Hints for Challenge Question 49: Scrap Rate

Key Table: Production.WorkOrder
Key Table: Production.ScrapReason
Key Table: Production.Product

Hints for Challenge Question 50: Reasons

Key Table: Sales.SalesOrderHeaderSalesReason
Key Table: Sales.SalesReason

Hints for Challenge Question 51: Excess Inventory

Key Table: Sales.SpecialOffer
Key Table: Sales.SalesOrderDetail

Hints for Challenge Question 52: Pay Rate Changes

Key Table: HumanResources.EmployeePayHistory
Key Column: RateChangeDate

Hints for Challenge Question 53: Sales Order Counts

Key Table: Sales.SalesOrderHeader
Key Function: PIVOT

Hints for Challenge Question 54: Loyal Customers

Key Table: Sales.SalesOrderHeader
Key Function: NEWID

Hints for Challenge Question 55: Date Range Gaps

Key Function: LEAD
Key Function: DATEDIFF

SOLUTIONS TO CHALLENGE QUESTIONS

Solutions to challenge questions available for download at http://realsqlqueries.com.

Solution 1 to Challenge Question 1: Year over Year Comparisons

```
--DROP TABLE #data

SELECT
   SalesPersonID
   ,FY =           DATEPART (YEAR, DATEADD (MONTH, 6, OrderDate))
   ,FQ =           DATEPART (QUARTER, DATEADD (MONTH, 6, OrderDate))
   ,FQSales =      SUM (Subtotal)
INTO #data
FROM Sales.SalesOrderHeader
WHERE OnlineOrderFlag = 0
GROUP BY
   SalesPersonID
   ,DATEPART (YEAR, DATEADD (MONTH, 6, OrderDate))
   ,DATEPART (QUARTER, DATEADD (MONTH, 6, OrderDate))

SELECT
   N3.LastName
   ,N1.*
   ,SalesSameFQLastYr =   N2.FQSales
   ,Change =              N1.FQSales - N2.FQSales
   ,[%Change] =           ((N1.FQSales - N2.FQSales) / N2.FQSales) * 100
FROM #data N1
LEFT JOIN #Data N2
   ON N1.SalesPersonID = N2.SalesPersonID
      AND N1.FQ = N2.FQ
      AND N1.FY -1 = N2.FY
INNER JOIN Person.Person N3 ON N1.SalesPersonID = N3.BusinessEntityID
WHERE N1.FY = 2008
ORDER BY SalesPersonID, FY DESC, FQ DESC
```

Solution 2 to Challenge Question 1: Year over Year Comparisons

```sql
--DROP TABLE #data2

SELECT
   SalesPersonID
   ,FY =       DATEPART (YEAR, DATEADD (MONTH, 6, OrderDate))
   ,FQ =       DATEPART (QUARTER, DATEADD (MONTH, 6, OrderDate))
   ,FQSales = SUM (Subtotal)
INTO #data2
FROM Sales.SalesOrderHeader
WHERE OnlineOrderFlag = 0
GROUP BY
   SalesPersonID
   ,DATEPART (YEAR, DATEADD (MONTH, 6, OrderDate))
   ,DATEPART (QUARTER, DATEADD (MONTH, 6, OrderDate));

WITH Final AS
(SELECT
  N2.LastName
  ,N1.*
  ,SalesSameFQLastYr =
      LAG (FQSales, 4) OVER
                        (PARTITION BY
                           SalesPersonID ORDER BY FY, FQ)
  ,Change =
        N1.FQSales -
            LAG (FQSales, 4) OVER
                              (PARTITION BY
                                 SalesPersonID ORDER BY FY, FQ)

  ,[%Change] =
        ((N1.FQSales - LAG (FQSales, 4)
              OVER (PARTITION BY SalesPersonID ORDER BY FY, FQ))
                  / LAG (FQSales, 4)
                        OVER (PARTITION BY
                                 SalesPersonID ORDER BY FY, FQ)) * 100
FROM #data2 N1
INNER JOIN Person.Person N2 ON N1.SalesPersonID = N2.BusinessEntityID)

SELECT *
FROM Final
WHERE FY = 2008
ORDER BY SalesPersonID, FY DESC, FQ DESC
```

Solution to Challenge Question 2: The 2/22 Promotion

```sql
-- Part I

--DROP TABLE #data


SELECT
   N1.SalesOrderID
   ,ShipToState =           N4.Name
   ,OrderDate =             N1.OrderDate
   ,[HistoricalOrder$] =    N1.SubTotal
   ,HistoricalFreight =     N1.Freight

   ,PotentialPromoEffect =  CASE
                                WHEN N1.SubTotal > = 1700 AND N1.SubTotal < 2000
                                    THEN 'INCREASE ORDER TO $2,000 & PAY 22 CENTS
                                        FREIGHT'
                                WHEN N1.Subtotal > = 2000
                                    THEN 'NO ORDER CHANGE AND PAY 22 CENTS FREIGHT'
                                ELSE 'NO ORDER CHANGE & PAY HISTORICAL FREIGHT' END

   ,PotentialOrderGain =    CASE
                                WHEN N1.SubTotal > = 1700
                                    AND N1.SubTotal < 2000
                                    THEN 2000 - N1.SubTotal
                                ELSE 0 END

   ,PotentialFreightLoss =  CASE
                                WHEN N1.SubTotal > =  1700
                                    THEN 0.22 ELSE N1.Freight END
                            - N1.Freight

   ,[PromoNetGain/Loss] =   CASE
                                WHEN N1.SubTotal > = 1700
                                    AND N1.SubTotal < 2000
                                    THEN 2000 - N1.SubTotal
                                ELSE 0 END
                            + CASE
                                WHEN N1.SubTotal > =  1700
                                    THEN 0.22
                                ELSE N1.Freight END
                            - N1.Freight
INTO #data
FROM Sales.SalesOrderHeader N1
INNER JOIN Person.BusinessEntityAddress N2 ON N1.ShipToAddressID = N2.AddressID
INNER JOIN Person.[Address] N3 ON N2.AddressID = N3.AddressID
INNER JOIN Person.StateProvince N4 ON N3.StateProvinceID = N4.StateProvinceID
WHERE N4.Name = 'California'
    AND DATEPART (YEAR, DATEADD (MONTH, 6, N1.OrderDate)) = 2008
```

```sql
SELECT *
FROM #data


-- Part II
SELECT
    PotentialPromoEffect
    ,PotentialOrderGains   =    SUM (PotentialOrderGain)
    ,PotentialFreightLosses =   SUM (PotentialFreightLoss)
    ,OverallNet =               SUM ([PromoNetGain/Loss])
FROM #data
GROUP BY PotentialPromoEffect
```

Solution 1 to Challenge Question 3: Ten Million Dollar Benchmark

```
--DROP TABLE #Sales

SELECT
   FiscalYear      =    YEAR (DATEADD (MONTH, 6, OrderDate))
   ,OrderDate      =    CAST (OrderDate AS DATE)
   ,OrderNumber    =    ROW_NUMBER () OVER
                            (PARTITION BY YEAR (DATEADD (MONTH, 6, OrderDate))
                             ORDER BY OrderDate)
   ,SubTotal
   ,RunningTotal = CONVERT (FLOAT, NULL)
INTO #Sales
FROM Sales.SalesOrderHeader

UPDATE N1 SET
   RunningTotal =    (SELECT SUM (SubTotal)
                     FROM #Sales X1
                     WHERE N1.FiscalYear = X1.FiscalYear
                        AND X1.OrderNumber <= N1.OrderNumber)
FROM #Sales N1


--DROP TABLE #FindOrder

SELECT
   FiscalYear
   ,OrderNumberOver10M = (SELECT TOP 1 X1.OrderNumber
                         FROM #Sales X1
                         WHERE N1.FiscalYear = X1.FiscalYear
                            AND X1.RunningTotal >= 10000000
                         ORDER BY X1.RunningTotal)
INTO #FindOrder
FROM #Sales N1
GROUP BY N1.FiscalYear

SELECT
  N2.FiscalYear
  ,N2.OrderDate
  ,N2.OrderNumber
  ,N2.RunningTotal
FROM #FindOrder N1
INNER JOIN #Sales N2 ON N1.FiscalYear = N2.FiscalYear
         AND N1.OrderNumberOver10M = N2.OrderNumber
WHERE N1.FiscalYear IN (2007, 2008)
```

Solution 2 to Challenge Question 3: Ten Million Dollar Benchmark

```sql
WITH FY2007 AS
    (SELECT
        FY =            2007
        ,OrderDate =    CAST (OrderDate AS DATE)
        ,[OrderNumber] = ROW_NUMBER () OVER (ORDER BY SalesOrderID)

        ,RunningTotal = SUM (SubTotal) OVER (ORDER BY Orderdate
                            ROWS BETWEEN UNBOUNDED PRECEDING AND CURRENT ROW)
        FROM Sales.SalesOrderHeader
        WHERE DATEPART (YEAR, DATEADD (MONTH, 6, OrderDate)) = 2007)

    ,FY2008 AS
    (SELECT
        FY =            2008
        ,OrderDate =    CAST (OrderDate AS DATE)
        ,[OrderNumber] = ROW_NUMBER () OVER (ORDER BY SalesOrderID)

        ,RunningTotal = SUM (SubTotal) OVER (ORDER BY Orderdate
                            ROWS BETWEEN UNBOUNDED PRECEDING AND CURRENT ROW)
        FROM Sales.SalesOrderHeader
        WHERE DATEPART (YEAR, DATEADD (MONTH, 6, OrderDate)) = 2008)

SELECT TOP 1 * FROM FY2007 WHERE RunningTotal > = 10000000
UNION
SELECT TOP 1 * FROM FY2008 WHERE RunningTotal > = 10000000
```

Solution to Challenge Question 4: Upsell Tuesdays

```sql
SELECT
    DayCategory =       DATENAME (WEEKDAY, OrderDate)


    ,Revenue =          SUM (Subtotal)
    ,Orders =           COUNT (*)
    ,RevenuePerOrder =  SUM (Subtotal) / COUNT (*)

FROM Sales.SalesOrderHeader
WHERE YEAR (OrderDate) = 2008 AND OnlineOrderFlag = 0
GROUP BY DATENAME (WEEKDAY, OrderDate)
ORDER BY RevenuePerOrder DESC
```

Solution to Challenge Question 5: Expired Credit Cards

```sql
-- Part I

--DROP TABLE #data

SELECT
   N1.CreditCardID
   ,N1.CardType
   ,ExpDate =       EOMONTH (DATEFROMPARTS (N1.ExpYear, N1.ExpMonth, 1))
   ,LastOrderDate = CAST (N2.LastOrderDate AS DATE)
   ,[Orders<=Exp] = COUNT (DISTINCT N3.SalesOrderID)
   ,[Orders>Exp] =  COUNT (DISTINCT N4.SalesOrderID)
INTO #data
FROM Sales.CreditCard N1

LEFT JOIN (SELECT X1.CreditCardID, LastOrderDate = MAX (X1.OrderDate)
           FROM Sales.SalesOrderHeader X1
           GROUP BY X1.CreditCardID) N2 ON N1.CreditCardID = N2.CreditCardID

LEFT JOIN Sales.SalesOrderHeader N3 ON 1 = 1
   AND N1.CreditCardID = N3.CreditCardID
   AND N3.OrderDate < = EOMONTH (DATEFROMPARTS (N1.ExpYear, N1.ExpMonth, 1))

LEFT JOIN Sales.SalesOrderHeader N4 ON 1 = 1
   AND N1.CreditCardID = N4.CreditCardID
   AND N4.OrderDate >  EOMONTH (DATEFROMPARTS (N1.ExpYear, N1.ExpMonth, 1))

GROUP BY
   N1.CreditCardID
   ,N1.CardType
   ,N2.LastOrderDate
   ,N1.ExpYear
   ,N1.ExpMonth

SELECT *
FROM #data
ORDER BY [Orders>Exp] DESC


--Part II
SELECT
   CardType
   ,[Orders<=Exp] = SUM ([Orders<=Exp])
   ,[Orders>Exp] =  SUM ([Orders>Exp])
FROM #data
GROUP BY CardType
```

Solution to Challenge Question 6: Print Catalog

```
SELECT
   N1.ProductID
   ,ProductName =   N1.Name
   ,N1.Color
   ,N1.ListPrice
   ,N2.TotalQty
FROM Production.Product N1
INNER JOIN (SELECT
            ProductID
            ,TotalQty = SUM (Quantity)
        FROM Production.ProductInventory
        GROUP BY ProductID) N2 ON N1.ProductID = N2.ProductID
WHERE N1.SellEndDate IS NULL
    AND N2.TotalQty > = 150
    AND N1.ListPrice > = 1500
    AND N1.FinishedGoodsFlag = 1
```

Solution 1 to Challenge Questions 7: Special Offers

```
SELECT
   N1.SpecialOfferID
   ,N1.[Description]
   ,N1.EndDate
FROM Sales.SpecialOffer N1
LEFT JOIN Sales.SpecialOfferProduct N2
   ON N1.SpecialOfferID = N2.SpecialOfferID
WHERE N2.SpecialOfferID IS NULL
   AND N1.DiscountPct > 0
   AND N1.EndDate > '2008-01-01'
```

Solution 2 to Challenge Questions 7: Special Offers

```
SELECT
   SpecialOfferID
   ,[Description]
   ,EndDate
FROM Sales.SpecialOffer N1
WHERE N1.DiscountPct > 0
   AND N1.EndDate > '2008-01-01'
   AND NOT EXISTS (SELECT 1
                   FROM Sales.SpecialOfferProduct X1
                   WHERE N1.SpecialOfferID = X1.SpecialOfferID)
```

Solution 3 to Challenge Questions 7: Special Offers

```
WITH [Data] AS
   (SELECT SpecialOfferID
    FROM Sales.SpecialOffer
    WHERE DiscountPct > 0
      AND EndDate > '2008-01-01'

    EXCEPT

    SELECT SpecialOfferID
    FROM Sales.SpecialOfferProduct)

SELECT
   N1.SpecialOfferID
   ,N1.[Description]
   ,N1.EndDate
FROM Sales.SpecialOffer N1
INNER JOIN [Data] N2 ON N1.SpecialOfferID = N2.SpecialOfferID
```

Solution to Challenge Question 8: Similar Products

```sql
DECLARE @Today DATE = '2014-01-01';

WITH [Data] AS

(SELECT
   Base_ProdID =       N1.ProductID
   ,Base_Prod_Name =   N1.[Name]
   ,Base_Prod_Price =  N1.ListPrice

   ,Similar_Product_ID = (SELECT TOP 1 ProductID
                          FROM Production.Product X1
                          WHERE N1.ProductSubcategoryID = X1.ProductSubcategoryID
                              AND N1.Size = X1.Size
                              AND N1.Style = X1.Style
                              AND X1.ListPrice < N1.ListPrice
                              AND X1.FinishedGoodsFlag = 1
                              AND X1.SellStartDate <= @Today
                              AND ISNULL (X1.SellEndDate, '9999-12-31') > @Today
                          ORDER BY X1.ListPrice DESC)

FROM Production.Product N1
WHERE N1.FinishedGoodsFlag = 1
   AND N1.SellStartDate <= @Today
   AND ISNULL (N1.SellEndDate, '9999-12-31') > @Today)

SELECT
   N1.Base_ProdID
   ,N1.Base_Prod_Name
   ,N1.Base_Prod_Price
   ,Similar_Prod_Price = N2.ListPrice
   ,Similar_Prod_Name =  N2.[Name]
   ,Similar_Product_ID
FROM [Data] N1
INNER JOIN Production.Product N2 ON N1.Similar_Product_ID = N2.ProductID
ORDER BY Base_ProdID
```

Solution to Challenge Question 9: Product Combinations

```sql
-- Temp table to be utilized throughout all parts of the solution

--DROP TABLE #ProductSales

SELECT
   N1.CustomerID
   ,N1.SalesOrderID
   ,ProductType =     N5.Name
   ,N3.ProductLine
   ,N3.ProductID
INTO #ProductSales
FROM Sales.SalesOrderHeader N1
INNER JOIN Sales.SalesOrderDetail N2 ON N1.SalesOrderID = N2.SalesOrderID
INNER JOIN Production.Product N3 ON N2.ProductID = N3.ProductID
INNER JOIN Production.ProductSubcategory N4
   ON N3.ProductSubcategoryID = N4.ProductSubcategoryID
INNER JOIN Production.ProductCategory N5
   ON N4.ProductCategoryID = N5.ProductCategoryID

-- Part I
DECLARE @TotalOrders FLOAT
   = (SELECT COUNT (DISTINCT SalesOrderID)
      FROM #ProductSales)

DECLARE @BikeAccessoryOrders FLOAT
   = (SELECT COUNT (DISTINCT N1.SalesOrderID)
      FROM #ProductSales N1
      INNER JOIN #ProductSales N2 ON N1.SalesOrderID = N2.SalesOrderID
      WHERE N1.ProductType = 'Bikes'
         AND N2.ProductType = 'Accessories')

SELECT BikeAndAccessory
   = CONVERT (VARCHAR(10),
         CONVERT (DECIMAL (5,2),
            (@BikeAccessoryOrders / @TotalOrders) * 100)) + ' %'

DECLARE @BikeClothingOrders FLOAT
   = (SELECT COUNT (*)
      FROM (SELECT SalesOrderID
            FROM #ProductSales
            GROUP BY SalesOrderID
            HAVING SUM (CASE WHEN ProductType = 'Bikes' THEN 1 ELSE 0 END) > = 1
               AND SUM (CASE WHEN ProductType = 'Clothing' THEN 1 ELSE 0 END) > = 2)
      X1)

SELECT BikeAndClothing = CONVERT (VARCHAR(10),
                     CONVERT (DECIMAL (5,2),
                        (@BikeClothingOrders / @TotalOrders) * 100)) + ' %'
```

```sql
-- Part II

--DROP TABLE #Pivot

SELECT *
INTO #Pivot
FROM (SELECT DISTINCT SalesOrderID, ProductType, Cnt = 1
    FROM #ProductSales) N1
PIVOT (COUNT (Cnt)
    FOR ProductType IN ([Bikes], [Accessories], [Clothing], [Components])
    ) X1

SELECT Bikes, Accessories, Clothing, Components, Orders = COUNT(*)
FROM #Pivot
GROUP BY Bikes, Accessories, Clothing, Components
ORDER BY Bikes, Accessories, Clothing, Components

-- Part III

--DROP TABLE #Pivot2

SELECT *
INTO #Pivot2
FROM (SELECT DISTINCT CustomerID, ProductLine, Cnt = 1
    FROM #ProductSales) N1
PIVOT (COUNT (Cnt)
    FOR ProductLine IN ([M],[S],[T],[R])) X1

SELECT M, S, T, R, Customers = COUNT (*)
FROM #Pivot2
GROUP BY M, S, T, R
ORDER BY M, S, T, R
```

Solution 1 to Challenge Question 10: Median Revenue

```sql
--DROP TABLE #Sales

SELECT
    OrderYear =             YEAR (OrderDate)
    ,SubTotal
    ,RowNumbForMedian =     ROW_NUMBER () OVER (PARTITION BY YEAR (OrderDate)
                                                ORDER BY SubTotal)
INTO #Sales
FROM Sales.SalesOrderHeader

--DROP TABLE #SalesGrouped

SELECT
    OrderYear
    ,NumbOrders=            COUNT (*)
    ,NumbOrdersEven =       CASE WHEN COUNT (*) % 2 = 0 THEN 1 ELSE 0 END
    ,FindMedian=            (COUNT (*) / 2) + 1
    ,Median =               CONVERT (FLOAT, NULL)
INTO #SalesGrouped
FROM #Sales
GROUP BY OrderYear

UPDATE N1 SET
    Median = N2.SubTotal
FROM #SalesGrouped N1
INNER JOIN #Sales N2 ON N1.OrderYear = N2.OrderYear
                    AND N1.FindMedian = N2.RowNumbForMedian
WHERE NumbOrdersEven = 0

UPDATE N1 SET
    Median =    (SELECT AVG (SubTotal)
                FROM #Sales X1
                WHERE N1.OrderYear = X1.OrderYear
                    AND X1.RowNumbForMedian IN (N1.FindMedian, (N1.FindMedian - 1)))
FROM #SalesGrouped N1
WHERE NumbOrdersEven = 1

SELECT
    N1.OrderYear
    ,MinSale =      MIN (SubTotal)
    ,MaxSale =      MAX (SubTotal)
    ,AvgSale =      AVG (SubTotal)
    ,MedianSale = N2.Median
FROM #Sales N1
INNER JOIN #SalesGrouped N2 ON N1.OrderYear = N2.OrderYear
GROUP BY N1.OrderYear, N2.Median
ORDER BY N1.OrderYear
```

Solution 2 to Challenge Question 10: Median Revenue

```sql
WITH MedianSales AS
   (SELECT DISTINCT
      OrderYear =    YEAR (OrderDate)
      ,MedianSale = PERCENTILE_DISC (0.5) WITHIN GROUP (ORDER BY Subtotal)
                    OVER (PARTITION BY YEAR (OrderDate))
   FROM Sales.SalesOrderHeader)

SELECT
   OrderYear =   YEAR (N1.OrderDate)
   ,MinSale =    MIN (N1.SubTotal)
   ,MaxSale =    MAX (N1.SubTotal)
   ,AvgSale =    AVG (N1.SubTotal)
   ,N2.MedianSale
FROM Sales.SalesOrderHeader N1
INNER JOIN MedianSales N2 ON YEAR (N1.OrderDate) = N2.OrderYear
GROUP BY YEAR (N1.OrderDate), N2.MedianSale
ORDER BY YEAR (N1.OrderDate)
```

Solution to Challenge Question 11: Needy Accountant

```sql
SELECT
   Country =       N3.Name
   ,MaxTaxRate =   MAX (N1.TaxRate)
FROM Sales.SalesTaxRate N1
INNER JOIN Person.StateProvince N2 ON N1.StateProvinceID = N2.StateProvinceID
INNER JOIN Person.CountryRegion N3 ON N2.CountryRegionCode = N3.CountryRegionCode
GROUP BY N3.Name
```

Solution to Challenge Question 12: Product Inventory Updates

```
CREATE VIEW Production.Vw_Product_Inventory

AS

SELECT
   LocationID =           CASE
                              WHEN GROUPING (LocationID) = 1
                                 THEN CONVERT (VARCHAR (5), 'Total')
                              ELSE CONVERT (VARCHAR (5), LocationID)
                          END

   ,DistinctProducts =    COUNT (DISTINCT ProductID)
   ,Quantity =            SUM (Quantity)
FROM Production.ProductInventory
GROUP BY LocationID WITH ROLLUP
```

Solution to Challenge Question 13: Vacation Hours

```
WITH MaxVacHrs AS

   (SELECT MaxVacHrs = MAX (VacationHours) FROM HumanResources.Employee)

SELECT
   NationalID =  RIGHT (N1.NationalIDNumber, 4)
   ,N2.FirstName
   ,N2.LastName
   ,N1.JobTitle
   ,N1.VacationHours
FROM HumanResources.Employee N1
INNER JOIN Person.Person N2 ON N1.BusinessEntityID = N2.BusinessEntityID
INNER JOIN MaxVacHrs N3 ON N1.VacationHours = N3.MaxVacHrs
```

Solution to Challenge Question 14: Purchasing

```
SELECT
   N1.ProductID
   ,ProductName =      N2.Name
   ,N3.OrderDate
   ,QuantityOrdered = SUM (N1.OrderQty)
FROM Purchasing.PurchaseOrderDetail N1
INNER JOIN Production.Product N2 ON N1.ProductID = N2.ProductID
INNER JOIN Purchasing.PurchaseOrderHeader N3
   ON N1.PurchaseOrderID = N3.PurchaseOrderID
WHERE YEAR (N3.OrderDate) = 2007
GROUP BY N1.Productid, N2.Name, N3.OrderDate
ORDER BY SUM (N1.OrderQty) DESC
```

Solution to Challenge Question 15: Interpretation Needed

```
SELECT
   N2.ProductModelID
   ,ProductModel =    N3.Name
   ,N1.[Description]
   ,[Language] =      N4.Name
FROM Production.ProductDescription N1
INNER JOIN Production.ProductModelProductDescriptionCulture N2
   ON N1.ProductDescriptionID = N2.ProductDescriptionID
INNER JOIN Production.ProductModel N3 ON N2.ProductModelID = N3.ProductModelID
INNER JOIN Production.Culture N4 ON N2.CultureID = N4.CultureID
WHERE N4.Name <> 'English'
```

Solution to Challenge Question 16: Online/Offline

```sql
SELECT
   TerritoryID
   ,TotalOrders =   COUNT (*)
   ,PercOnline =    CONVERT (VARCHAR (50),
                      ROUND(
                         (CONVERT (FLOAT,
                            SUM (CASE WHEN OnlineOrderFlag = 1 THEN 1 ELSE 0 END))
                            / COUNT(*))
                            * 100
                        ,0)
                      ) + '%'
   ,PercOffline =   CONVERT(VARCHAR(50),
                      ROUND(
                         (CONVERT(FLOAT,
                            SUM (CASE WHEN OnlineOrderFlag = 0 THEN 1 ELSE 0 END))
                            /COUNT(*))
                            * 100
                        ,0)
                      ) + '%'
FROM Sales.SalesOrderHeader
GROUP BY TerritoryID
ORDER BY TerritoryID
```

Solution to Challenge Question 17: Long Time No Sale

```sql
WITH Stores AS
   (SELECT
      N3.BusinessEntityID
      ,N1.CustomerID
      ,N2.StoreID
      ,StoreName =            N3.Name
      ,LastOrderDate =        MAX (N1.OrderDate)
      ,MonthsSinceLastOrder = DATEDIFF (MONTH, MAX (N1.OrderDate), '2008-10-07')
FROM Sales.SalesOrderHeader N1
INNER JOIN Sales.Customer N2 ON N1.CustomerID = N2.CustomerID
INNER JOIN Sales.Store N3 ON N2.StoreID = N3.BusinessEntityID
GROUP BY N3.BusinessEntityID, N2.StoreID, N1.CustomerID, N3.Name)

SELECT *
FROM Stores
WHERE MonthsSinceLastOrder >= 12
ORDER BY MonthsSinceLastOrder DESC
```

Solution to Challenge Question 18: Costs Vary

```
SELECT
  N1.ProductID
  ,ProductName =    N2.Name
  ,SubCategory =    N3.Name
  ,MinCost =        MIN (N1.StandardCost)
  ,MaxCost =        MAX (N1.StandardCost)
  ,CostVar =        MAX (N1.StandardCost) - MIN (N1.StandardCost)

  ,CostVarRank =    CASE
                        WHEN MAX (N1.StandardCost) - MIN (N1.StandardCost) = 0 THEN 0
                        ELSE DENSE_RANK () OVER (ORDER BY
                            MAX (N1.StandardCost) - MIN (N1.StandardCost)  DESC)
                    END

FROM Production.ProductCostHistory N1
INNER JOIN Production.Product N2
  ON N1.ProductID = N2.ProductID
INNER JOIN Production.ProductSubcategory N3
  ON N2.ProductSubcategoryID = N3.ProductSubcategoryID
GROUP BY N1.ProductID, N2.Name, N3.Name
ORDER BY CostVar DESC
```

Solution to Challenge Question 19: Thermoform Temperature

```sql
WITH Temp AS
   (SELECT
       RNK =              ROW_NUMBER () OVER (PARTITION BY N1.ProductID
                                              ORDER BY COUNT (N2.Name) DESC)
      ,N1.ProductID
      ,ProductName =    N2.Name
      ,WorkOrderCount = COUNT (N2.Name)
      ,ScrapReason =    N3.Name
    FROM Production.WorkOrder N1
    INNER JOIN Production.Product N2 ON N1.ProductID = N2.ProductID
    INNER JOIN Production.ScrapReason N3 ON N1.ScrapReasonID = N3.ScrapReasonID
    GROUP BY N1.ProductID, N2.Name, N3.Name)

SELECT
   ProductID
  ,ProductName
  ,WorkOrderCount
  ,ScrapReason
FROM Temp
WHERE RNK = 1
ORDER BY WorkOrderCount DESC
```

Solution to Challenge Question 20: Toronto

```
SELECT
   AddressType=    N3.Name
   ,StoreName =    N4.Name
   ,N2.AddressLine1
   ,N2.AddressLine2
   ,N2.City
   ,StateProvince = N5.Name
   ,N2.PostalCode
FROM Person.BusinessEntityAddress N1
INNER JOIN Person.[Address] N2 ON N1.AddressID = N2.AddressID
INNER JOIN Person.AddressType N3 ON N1.AddressTypeID = N3.AddressTypeID
INNER JOIN Sales.Store N4 ON N1.BusinessEntityID = N4.BusinessEntityID
INNER JOIN Person.StateProvince N5 ON N2.StateProvinceID = N5.StateProvinceID
WHERE N3.Name = 'Main office' and N2.City = 'Toronto'
```

Solution to Challenge Question 21: Marketing Employees

```
SELECT
   N3.FirstName
   ,N3.LastName
   ,N4.JobTitle
   ,N4.BirthDate
   ,N4.MaritalStatus
   ,N4.HireDate
FROM HumanResources.EmployeeDepartmentHistory N1
INNER JOIN HumanResources.Department N2 ON N1.DepartmentID = N2.DepartmentID
INNER JOIN Person.Person N3 ON N1.BusinessEntityID = N3.BusinessEntityID
INNER JOIN HumanResources.Employee N4 ON N1.BusinessEntityID = N4.BusinessEntityID
WHERE N2.Name = 'Marketing'
      AND ((YEAR (N4.HireDate) < 2002) OR YEAR (N4.HireDate) > 2004)
      AND N1.EndDate IS NULL
```

Solution to Challenge Question 22: Who Left That Review?

```sql
SELECT
   N1.ProductReviewID
   ,N1.ProductID
   ,ProductName =    N2.Name
   ,N1.ReviewerName
   ,N1.Rating
   ,ReviewerEmail =    N1.EmailAddress
   ,N3.BusinessEntityID
FROM Production.ProductReview N1
INNER JOIN Production.Product N2 ON N1.ProductID = N2.ProductID
LEFT JOIN Person.EmailAddress N3 ON N1.EmailAddress = N3.EmailAddress

--Execution returns each BusinessEntityID as NULL. It will not be possible to locate
sales orders related to product reviews because there are no matches.
```

Solution to Challenge Question 23: Label Mix-Up

```sql
SELECT
   N1.SalesOrderID
   ,N3.OrderDate
   ,ProductName =    N2.Name
   ,N5.FirstName
   ,N5.LastName
   ,N6.PhoneNumber
FROM Sales.SalesOrderDetail N1
INNER JOIN Production.Product N2 ON N1.ProductID = N2.ProductID
INNER JOIN Sales.SalesOrderHeader N3 ON N1.SalesOrderID = N3.SalesOrderID
INNER JOIN Sales.Customer N4 ON N3.CustomerID = N4.CustomerID
INNER JOIN Person.Person N5 ON N4.PersonID = N5.BusinessEntityID
INNER JOIN Person.PersonPhone N6 ON N5.BusinessEntityID = N6.BusinessEntityID
WHERE N2.Name like '%shorts%'
      AND N3.OrderDate > '2008-07-07'
      AND N3.OnlineOrderFlag = 1
ORDER BY SalesOrderID
```

Solution to Challenge Question 24: Clearance Sale

```sql
WITH Email AS
   (SELECT
      N1.BusinessEntityID
      ,N1.EmailAddress
      ,EmailPref =
         CASE
            WHEN N2.EmailPromotion = 0 THEN
               'Contact does not wish to receive e-mail promotions'
            WHEN N2.EmailPromotion = 1 THEN
               'Contact does wish to receive e-mail promotions from AdventureWorks'
            WHEN N2.EmailPromotion = 2 THEN
               'Contact does wish to receive e-mail promotions from
               AdventureWorks and selected partners'
         END
FROM Person.EmailAddress N1
LEFT JOIN Person.Person N2 ON N1.BusinessEntityID = N2.BusinessEntityID
WHERE N2.PersonType = 'IN')

SELECT
   EmailPref
   ,[Count] = COUNT (*)
FROM Email
GROUP BY EmailPref
ORDER BY [Count] DESC
```

Solution to Challenge Question 25: Top Territories

```
WITH TerritoryRank AS

(SELECT
   FY =                  YEAR (DATEADD (MONTH, 6, N1.OrderDate))
   ,Territory =          N2.Name
   ,Revenue =            SUM (N1.SubTotal)
   ,[Territory$Rank] =   DENSE_RANK () OVER (
                         PARTITION BY YEAR (DATEADD (MONTH, 6, N1.OrderDate))
                         ORDER BY SUM (N1.Subtotal) DESC)
FROM Sales.SalesOrderHeader N1
INNER JOIN Sales.SalesTerritory N2 ON N1.TerritoryID = N2.TerritoryID
GROUP BY YEAR (DATEADD (MONTH, 6, N1.OrderDate)), N2.Name)

SELECT *
FROM TerritoryRank
WHERE FY IN (2006, 2007) AND Territory$Rank IN (1, 2)
ORDER BY FY, Territory$Rank
```

Solution to Challenge Question 26: Commission Percentages

```
SELECT
   BusinessEntityID
   ,CommissionPct
   ,Bonus
   ,[Rank] =  DENSE_RANK () OVER (ORDER BY CommissionPct DESC, Bonus DESC)
FROM Sales.SalesPerson
ORDER BY CommissionPct DESC
```

Solution to Challenge Question 27: Work Orders

```sql
-- Part I
SELECT
    ProductID
    ,WorkOrders = COUNT (*)
FROM Production.WorkOrder
GROUP BY ProductID
ORDER BY COUNT (*) DESC

-- Part II
SELECT
    ProductName = N2.Name
    ,WorkOrders = COUNT (*)
FROM Production.WorkOrder N1
INNER JOIN Production.Product N2 ON N1.ProductID = N2.ProductID
GROUP BY N2.Name
ORDER BY COUNT (*) DESC
```

Solution to Challenge Question 28: Revenue Trended

```
DECLARE @StartDate DATE = '2008-05-01'
DECLARE @EndDate DATE = '2008-05-23'

-- Part I:
SELECT
   DaysInMonthSoFar =         DATEDIFF (day, @StartDate, @EndDate) + 1
   ,RevenueInMonthSoFar =     SUM (SubTotal)
   ,RevPerDayforMonthSoFar =  (SUM (SubTotal) /
                              (DATEDIFF (day, @StartDate, @EndDate) + 1))
   ,DaysInMonth =             DAY (EOMONTH (@StartDate))
   ,MonthlyRevTrended =       SUM (SubTotal) /
                              (DATEDIFF (day, @StartDate, @EndDate) + 1)
                              * DAY (EOMONTH (@StartDate))
FROM Sales.SalesOrderHeader
WHERE OrderDate BETWEEN @StartDate AND @EndDate

-- Part II:
SELECT
   ActualPerDay =   SUM (SubTotal) / DAY (EOMONTH (@StartDate))
   ,ActualRev =     SUM (Subtotal)
FROM Sales.SalesOrderHeader
WHERE OrderDate BETWEEN @StartDate AND EOMONTH (@EndDate)
```

Solution to Challenge Question 29: Separation

```
SELECT
   BusinessEntityID
   ,LoginID
   ,Domain =     LEFT (LoginID, CHARINDEX ('\', LoginID, 1) - 1)
   ,UserName =   RIGHT (LoginID, LEN (LoginID) - CHARINDEX ('\', LoginID, 1))
FROM HumanResources.Employee
ORDER BY BusinessEntityID
```

Solution to Challenge Question 30: Shift Coverage

```
SELECT
   DepartmentName = N2.Name
   ,ShiftName =    N3.Name
   ,Employees =    COUNT (*)
FROM HumanResources.EmployeeDepartmentHistory N1
INNER JOIN HumanResources.Department N2 ON N1.DepartmentID = N2.DepartmentID
INNER JOIN HumanResources.[Shift] N3 ON N1.ShiftID = N3.ShiftID
WHERE N2.Name = 'Production'
   AND N1.EndDate IS NULL
GROUP BY N2.Name, N3.Name
ORDER BY N2.Name, N3.Name
```

Solution to Challenge Question 31: Labels

```
-- Part I
SELECT DISTINCT Size
FROM Production.Product
WHERE ISNUMERIC (Size) = 0
   AND Size IS NOT NULL

-- The variety of stickers is appropriate for assignment to the company's products.


-- Part II
SELECT
   N1.Size
   ,CurrentQty =           SUM (N2.Quantity)

   ,AdditLabelsNeeded =    CASE
                              WHEN SUM (N2.Quantity) - 1000 < 0
                                 THEN 0
                              ELSE SUM (N2.Quantity) - 1000
                           END

FROM Production.Product N1
INNER JOIN Production.ProductInventory N2 ON N1.ProductID = N2.ProductID
WHERE ISNUMERIC (N1.Size) = 0
   AND N1.Size IS NOT NULL
GROUP BY N1.Size
```

Solution to Challenge Question 32: Employment Survey

```sql
-- Part I
SELECT
    Employees =     COUNT (*)
   ,[%Male] =       ROUND (SUM (CASE WHEN Gender = 'M' THEN 1 ELSE 0 END) /
                           CONVERT (FLOAT, COUNT (*)) * 100, 2)
   ,[%Female] =     ROUND (SUM (CASE WHEN Gender = 'F' THEN 1 ELSE 0 END) /
                           CONVERT (FLOAT, COUNT (*)) * 100, 2)
   ,AvgMonthsEmp = AVG (DATEDIFF (MONTH, HireDate, '2008-01-01'))
FROM HumanResources.Employee

-- Part II
SELECT
    X1.Quartile
   ,Employees =     COUNT (*)
   ,[%Male] =       ROUND (SUM (CASE WHEN X1.Gender = 'M' THEN 1 ELSE 0 END) /
                           CONVERT (FLOAT, COUNT (*)) * 100, 2)
   ,[%Female] =     ROUND (SUM (CASE WHEN X1.Gender = 'F' THEN 1 ELSE 0 END) /
                           CONVERT (FLOAT, COUNT (*)) * 100, 2)
   ,AvgMonthsEmp = AVG (X1.MonthsEmployed)
FROM (SELECT
        BusinessEntityID
       ,Quartile =      NTILE (4) OVER (ORDER BY DATEDIFF (
                                    MONTH, HireDate, '2008-01-01'))
       ,HireDate
       ,MonthsEmployed = DATEDIFF (MONTH, HireDate, '2008-01-01')
       ,Gender
      FROM HumanResources.Employee) X1
GROUP BY X1.Quartile
```

Solution to Challenge Question 33: Age Groups

```sql
SELECT
   N1.JobTitle
   ,AgeGroup =      CASE
                        WHEN DATEDIFF (YY, N1.BirthDate, '2008-01-01') < 18
                           THEN '< 18'
                        WHEN DATEDIFF (YY, N1.BirthDate, '2008-01-01') < 35
                           THEN '18 - 35'
                        WHEN DATEDIFF (YY, N1.BirthDate, '2008-01-01') < 50
                           THEN '36 - 50'
                        WHEN DATEDIFF (YY, N1.BirthDate, '2008-01-01') < 60
                           THEN '51 - 60'
                        ELSE '61 +'
                    END
   ,N2.Rate
   ,Employees =  COUNT (N1.BusinessEntityID)
FROM HumanResources.Employee N1
INNER JOIN HumanResources.EmployeePayHistory N2
   ON N1.BusinessEntityID = N2.BusinessEntityID
INNER JOIN (SELECT BusinessEntityID, RatechangeDate = MAX (RateChangeDate)
            FROM HumanResources.EmployeePayHistory
            GROUP BY BusinessEntityID) N3
   ON N3.BusinessEntityID = N2.BusinessEntityID
      AND N3.RatechangeDate = N2.RateChangeDate

GROUP BY
   JobTitle
   ,Rate
   ,CASE
      WHEN DATEDIFF (YY, N1.BirthDate, '2008-01-01') < 18 THEN '< 18'
      WHEN DATEDIFF (YY, N1.BirthDate, '2008-01-01') < 35 THEN '18 - 35'
      WHEN DATEDIFF (YY, N1.BirthDate, '2008-01-01') < 50 THEN '36 - 50'
      WHEN DATEDIFF (YY, N1.BirthDate, '2008-01-01') < 60 THEN '51 - 60'
      ELSE '61 +'
   END
```

Solution to Challenge Question 34: Revenue by State

```sql
SELECT
   [State] =     N3.Name
   ,TotalSales = SUM (N1.TotalDue)
FROM Sales.SalesOrderHeader N1
INNER JOIN Person.[Address] N2 ON N1.ShipToAddressID = N2.AddressID
INNER JOIN Person.StateProvince N3 ON N2.StateProvinceID = N3.StateProvinceID
WHERE YEAR (N1.OrderDate) = 2006
GROUP BY N3.Name
ORDER BY SUM (N1.TotalDue) DESC
```

Solution to Challenge Question 35: Two Free Bikes

```sql
--DROP VIEW HumanResources.Vw_Employee_Bicycle_Giveaway

CREATE VIEW HumanResources.Vw_Employee_Bicycle_Giveaway

AS

SELECT TOP 2
   N2.FirstName
   ,N2.LastName
   ,N1.JobTitle
FROM HumanResources.Employee N1
INNER JOIN Person.Person N2 ON N1.BusinessEntityID = N2.BusinessEntityID
WHERE N1.OrganizationLevel = (SELECT MAX (OrganizationLevel)
                              FROM HumanResources.Employee)
ORDER BY NEWID ()
```

Solution to Challenge Question 36: Volume Discounts

```sql
--DROP TABLE #data

SELECT
   N1.SalesOrderID
   ,N3.OrderDate
   ,TotalVolumeDiscount = SUM (N1.UnitPriceDiscount * N1.UnitPrice * N1.OrderQty)
INTO #data
FROM Sales.SalesOrderDetail N1
INNER JOIN Sales.SpecialOffer N2 ON N1.SpecialOfferID = N2.SpecialOfferID
INNER JOIN Sales.SalesOrderHeader N3 ON N1.SalesOrderID = N3.SalesOrderID
WHERE N2.[Type] = 'Volume Discount'
GROUP BY N1.SalesOrderID, N2.[Type], N3.OrderDate
HAVING SUM (N1.UnitPriceDiscount * N1.UnitPrice * N1.OrderQty) > 0

-- Part I
SELECT *
FROM #data
ORDER BY SalesOrderID

-- Part II
SELECT
   OrderYear =            YEAR (OrderDate)
   ,TotalVolumeDiscount = SUM (TotalVolumeDiscount)
FROM #data
GROUP BY YEAR (OrderDate)
```

Solution to Challenge Question 37: Overpaying

```sql
--DROP TABLE #ProductVendor

SELECT
   ProductID
  ,MostExpensivePrice =        MAX (LastReceiptCost)
  ,SecondMostExpensivePrice = CONVERT (FLOAT,NULL)
  ,PercOverSecondPrice =       CONVERT (FLOAT,NULL)
INTO #ProductVendor
FROM Purchasing.ProductVendor
GROUP BY ProductID
HAVING COUNT (DISTINCT LastReceiptCost) > 1

UPDATE N1
   SET SecondMostExpensivePrice = (SELECT TOP 1 X1.LastReceiptCost
                                   FROM Purchasing.ProductVendor X1
                                   WHERE N1.ProductID = X1.ProductID
                                     AND N1.MostExpensivePrice <> X1.LastReceiptCost
                                   ORDER BY X1.LastReceiptCost DESC)
FROM #ProductVendor N1

UPDATE N1
   SET PercOverSecondPrice = CONVERT (DECIMAL (10,2),
                               CONVERT (FLOAT,
                                  (MostExpensivePrice - SecondMostExpensivePrice))
                                   / SecondMostExpensivePrice)
FROM #ProductVendor N1


SELECT *
FROM #ProductVendor
ORDER BY PercOverSecondPrice DESC
```

Solution to Challenge Question 38: Margins

```
SELECT
   N1.ProductModelID
   ,ProductName =      N4.Name
   ,ProfitMargin =     CONVERT (DECIMAL(10,2),
                           CONVERT (FLOAT,
                                    (N1.ListPrice - N1.StandardCost)) /
                                    N1.StandardCost)
FROM Production.Product N1
INNER JOIN Production.ProductSubcategory N2
   ON N1.ProductSubcategoryID = N2.ProductSubcategoryID
INNER JOIN Production.ProductCategory N3
   ON N2.ProductCategoryID = N3.ProductCategoryID
INNER JOIN Production.ProductModel N4
   ON N1.ProductModelID = N4.ProductModelID
WHERE N3.Name = 'Bikes' AND N1.SellEndDate IS NULL
GROUP BY
   N1.ProductModelID
   ,N4.Name
   ,CONVERT (DECIMAL (10,2)
   ,CONVERT (FLOAT, (N1.ListPrice - N1.StandardCost)) / N1.StandardCost)
ORDER BY ProfitMargin DESC
```

Solution to Challenge Question 39: Percent to Quota

```sql
-- Part I

--DROP TABLE #SalesQuotaSummary

SELECT
    N1.BusinessEntityID
   ,N1.QuotaDate
   ,N1.SalesQuota
   ,ActualSales = CONVERT (DECIMAL (10,2), SUM (N2.SubTotal))
   ,PercToQuota = CONVERT (DECIMAL (10,2),
                  CONVERT (FLOAT, SUM (N2.SubTotal)) / N1.SalesQuota)
INTO #SalesQuotaSummary
FROM Sales.SalesPersonQuotaHistory N1
LEFT JOIN Sales.SalesOrderHeader N2 ON N1.BusinessEntityID = N2.SalesPersonID
                                  AND N2.OrderDate >= N1.QuotaDate
                                  AND N2.OrderDate < DATEADD (MONTH, 3, N1.QuotaDate)
GROUP BY
   N1.BusinessEntityID
  ,N1.QuotaDate
  ,N1.SalesQuota

SELECT *
FROM #SalesQuotaSummary
ORDER BY BusinessEntityID, QuotaDate

-- Part II
SELECT
   BusinessEntityID
  ,QuotaYear =          YEAR (QuotaDate)
  ,TotalQuota=          SUM (SalesQuota)
  ,TotalSales=          SUM (ActualSales)
  ,TotalPercToQuota =   CONVERT (DECIMAL (10,2),
                        CONVERT (FLOAT, SUM (ActualSales)) / SUM (SalesQuota))
  ,AvgQrtlyPercToQuota =CONVERT (DECIMAL (10,2), AVG (PercToQuota))
FROM #SalesQuotaSummary
GROUP BY BusinessEntityID, YEAR (QuotaDate)
ORDER BY BusinessEntityID, YEAR (QuotaDate)
```

Solution to Challenge Question 40: Revenue Ranges

```sql
SELECT
   SortID =                CASE
                              WHEN TotalDue < 100 THEN 1
                              WHEN TotalDue < 500 THEN 2
                              WHEN TotalDue < 1000 THEN 3
                              WHEN TotalDue < 2500 THEN 4
                              WHEN TotalDue < 5000 THEN 5
                              WHEN TotalDue < 10000 THEN 6
                              WHEN TotalDue < 50000 THEN 7
                              WHEN TotalDue < 100000 THEN 8
                              ELSE 9 END
   ,SalesAmountCategory =CASE
                              WHEN TotalDue < 100 THEN '0 - 100'
                              WHEN TotalDue < 500 THEN '100 - 500'
                              WHEN TotalDue < 1000 THEN '500 - 1,000'
                              WHEN TotalDue < 2500 THEN '1,000 - 2,500'
                              WHEN TotalDue < 5000 THEN '2,500 - 5,000'
                              WHEN TotalDue < 10000 THEN '5,000 - 10,000'
                              WHEN TotalDue < 50000 THEN '10,000 - 50,000'
                              WHEN TotalDue < 100000 THEN '50,000 - 100,000'
                              ELSE '> 100,000' END
   ,Orders =               COUNT (*)
FROM Sales.SalesOrderHeader
WHERE YEAR (OrderDate) = 2005
GROUP BY
   CASE
      WHEN TotalDue < 100 THEN 1
      WHEN TotalDue < 500 THEN 2
      WHEN TotalDue < 1000 THEN 3
      WHEN TotalDue < 2500 THEN 4
      WHEN TotalDue < 5000 THEN 5
      WHEN TotalDue < 10000 THEN 6
      WHEN TotalDue < 50000 THEN 7
      WHEN TotalDue < 100000 THEN 8
      ELSE 9 END
   ,CASE
      WHEN TotalDue < 100 THEN '0 - 100'
      WHEN TotalDue < 500 THEN '100 - 500'
      WHEN TotalDue < 1000 THEN '500 - 1,000'
      WHEN TotalDue < 2500 THEN '1,000 - 2,500'
      WHEN TotalDue < 5000 THEN '2,500 - 5,000'
      WHEN TotalDue < 10000 THEN '5,000 - 10,000'
      WHEN TotalDue < 50000 THEN '10,000 - 50,000'
      WHEN TotalDue < 100000 THEN '50,000 - 100,000'
      ELSE '> 100,000' END
ORDER BY SortID
```

Solution to Challenge Question 41: E-mail Mystery

```
SELECT
   N2.PersonType
  ,AWEmail =    SUM (CASE WHEN N1.EmailAddress LIKE '%adventure-works%'
                    THEN 1 ELSE 0 END)
  ,NotAWEmail = SUM (CASE WHEN N1.EmailAddress NOT LIKE '%adventure-works%'
                    THEN 1 ELSE 0 END)
  ,Total =      COUNT (*)
FROM Person.EmailAddress N1
INNER JOIN Person.Person N2 ON N1.BusinessEntityID = N2.BusinessEntityID
GROUP BY N2.PersonType
ORDER BY Total DESC
```

Solution to Challenge Question 42: The Mentors

```
WITH SalesGrouping AS
  (SELECT
      SalesPersonID
     ,SalesTotal =            SUM (SubTotal)
     ,SalesRankSubTotalDESC = ROW_NUMBER () OVER (ORDER BY SUM (Subtotal) DESC)
     ,SalesRankSubTotalASC =  ROW_NUMBER () OVER (ORDER BY SUM (Subtotal))
   FROM Sales.SalesOrderHeader
   WHERE YEAR (OrderDate) = 2008 AND SalesPersonID IS NOT NULL
   GROUP BY SalesPersonID)

SELECT TOP 5
    SuccessSalesPersonID =     N1.SalesPersonID
   ,SuccessRevenue =           N1.SalesTotal
   ,UnsuccessSalesPersonID =   N2.SalesPersonID
   ,UnsuccessRevenue =         N2.SalesTotal
FROM SalesGrouping N1
INNER JOIN SalesGrouping N2 ON N1.SalesRankSubTotalDESC = N2.SalesRankSubTotalASC
ORDER BY N1.SalesRankSubTotalDESC
```

Solution to Challenge Question 43: Calendar of Work Days

```sql
--DROP TABLE HumanResources.Calendar

CREATE TABLE HumanResources.Calendar
   (DateID INT
   ,[Date] DATETIME
   ,[Year] INT
   ,TextMonth VARCHAR (50)
   ,DateMonth DATETIME
   ,[DayOfWeek] VARCHAR (50)
   ,IsBusinessDay TINYINT)

DECLARE @StartDate DATETIME = '1990-01-01'
DECLARE @EndDate DATETIME = '2015-01-01'

DECLARE @TotalDays INT = DATEDIFF (DAY, @StartDate, @EndDate) + 1

DECLARE @Index INT = 1

WHILE @Index <= @TotalDays
BEGIN
   INSERT INTO HumanResources.Calendar (DateID)
   SELECT @Index
   SET @Index = @Index + 1
END

UPDATE N1
SET [Date] = DATEADD (DAY, DateID - 1, @StartDate)
FROM HumanResources.Calendar N1

UPDATE N1
   SET
      [Year] =          YEAR ([Date])
      ,TextMonth =      DATENAME (MONTH, [Date]) + ' ' + DATENAME (YEAR, [Date])
      ,DateMonth =      DATEADD (MONTH, DATEDIFF (MONTH, 0, [Date]), 0)
      ,[DayOfWeek] =    DATENAME (DW, [Date])
      ,IsBusinessDay = CASE WHEN DATENAME (DW, [Date]) IN ('Saturday', 'Sunday')
                       THEN 0 ELSE 1
                       END
FROM HumanResources.Calendar N1

SELECT
   [Year]
   ,BusinessDays = SUM (IsBusinessDay)
FROM HumanResources.Calendar
GROUP BY [Year]
ORDER BY [Year]
```

Solution to Challenge Question 44: Annual Salaries by Employee

```sql
--DROP TABLE #EmployeePayHistory

SELECT *
   ,BusinessEntityOrder = ROW_NUMBER () OVER (PARTITION BY BusinessEntityID
                                              ORDER BY RateChangeDate)

   ,RateEndDate =        CONVERT (DATETIME, NULL)
   ,BusinessDays =       CONVERT (INT, NULL)
INTO #EmployeePayHistory
FROM HumanResources.EmployeePayHistory

UPDATE N1
   SET   RateEndDate =   (SELECT TOP 1 RateChangeDate
                          FROM #EmployeePayHistory X1
                          WHERE N1.BusinessEntityID = X1.BusinessEntityID
                             AND X1.BusinessEntityOrder = N1.BusinessEntityOrder + 1
                          ORDER BY X1.RateChangeDate)
FROM #EmployeePayHistory N1


UPDATE N1
   SET BusinessDays =    (SELECT COUNT (*)
                          FROM HumanResources.Calendar X1
                          WHERE X1.[Date] BETWEEN N1.RateChangeDate
                             AND ISNULL (N1.RateEndDate, '2009-01-01')
                             AND X1.IsBusinessDay = 1)
FROM #EmployeePayHistory N1

--DROP TABLE #EmployeePayCalendar

SELECT *
   ,DailyPay = Rate * 8
INTO #EmployeePayCalendar
FROM #EmployeePayHistory N1
INNER JOIN HumanResources.Calendar N2
   ON N2.[Date] > = N1.RateChangeDate
      AND N2.[Date] < ISNULL (N1.RateEndDate, '2009-01-01')
      AND N2.IsBusinessDay = 1

SELECT
   BusinessEntityID
   ,WorkingYear =   [Year]
   ,TotalPay =      SUM (DailyPay)
FROM #EmployeePayCalendar
WHERE [Year] BETWEEN 2005 AND 2008
GROUP BY BusinessEntityID, [Year]
ORDER BY BusinessEntityID, [Year]
```

Solution to Challenge Question 45: Annual Salaries by Department

```sql
--DROP TABLE #EmployeePayDepartmentCalendar

SELECT
   N1.DepartmentID
   ,N1.StartDate
   ,N1.EndDate
   ,N2.*
INTO #EmployeePayDepartmentCalendar
FROM HumanResources.EmployeeDepartmentHistory N1
LEFT JOIN #EmployeePayCalendar N2 ON 1 = 1
        AND N1.BusinessEntityID = N2.BusinessEntityID
        AND N2.[Date] BETWEEN N1.StartDate AND ISNULL (N1.EndDate, '2009-01-01')

--DROP TABLE #DepartmentEmployeeSummary

SELECT
   DepartmentID
   ,BusinessEntityID
   ,TotalPay =      SUM (DailyPay)
INTO #DepartmentEmployeeSummary
FROM #EmployeePayDepartmentCalendar
WHERE [Year] = 2008
GROUP BY DepartmentID, BusinessEntityID

SELECT
   DepartmentID
   ,MinSalary = MIN (TotalPay)
   ,AvgSalary = AVG (TotalPay)
   ,MaxSalary = MAX (TotalPay)
FROM #DepartmentEmployeeSummary
GROUP BY DepartmentID
```

Solution 1 to Challenge Question 46: Holiday Bonus

```sql
SELECT
   N1.BusinessEntityID
   ,N2.FirstName
   ,N2.LastName
   ,N1.JobTitle

   ,Bonus    =      (SELECT TOP 1 Rate
                     FROM HumanResources.EmployeePayHistory X1
                     WHERE N1.BusinessEntityID = X1.BusinessEntityID
                     ORDER BY RateChangeDate DESC) * 50

FROM HumanResources.Employee N1
INNER JOIN Person.Person AS N2 ON N1.BusinessEntityID = N2.BusinessEntityID
WHERE N1.SalariedFlag = 1
ORDER BY N1.BusinessEntityID
```

Solution 2 to Challenge Question 46: Holiday Bonus

```sql
SELECT
   N1.BusinessEntityID
   ,N2.FirstName
   ,N2.LastName
   ,N1.JobTitle
   ,Bonus =       N3.Rate * 50
FROM HumanResources.Employee N1
INNER JOIN Person.Person AS N2 ON N1.BusinessEntityID = N2.BusinessEntityID
INNER JOIN HumanResources.EmployeePayHistory AS N3
   ON N1.BusinessEntityID = N3.BusinessEntityID
      AND N3.RateChangeDate = (SELECT MAX (RateChangeDate)
                               FROM HumanResources.EmployeePayHistory X1
                               WHERE N1.BusinessEntityID = X1.BusinessEntityID)
WHERE N1.SalariedFlag = 1
ORDER BY BusinessEntityID
```

Solution 3 to Challenge Question 46: Holiday Bonus

```
SELECT
   N1.BusinessEntityID
   ,N2.FirstName
   ,N2.LastName
   ,N1.JobTitle
   ,Bonus = N4.Rate * 50
FROM HumanResources.Employee N1
INNER JOIN Person.Person AS N2
   ON N1.BusinessEntityID = N2.BusinessEntityID
INNER JOIN
   (SELECT BusinessEntityID, MaxDate = MAX (RateChangeDate)
    FROM HumanResources.EmployeePayHistory
    GROUP BY BusinessEntityID) AS N3
   ON N1.BusinessEntityID = N3.BusinessEntityID
INNER JOIN HumanResources.EmployeePayHistory N4
   ON N3.MaxDate = N4.RateChangeDate
       AND N3.BusinessEntityID = N4.BusinessEntityID
WHERE SalariedFlag = 1
ORDER BY BusinessEntityID
```

Solution to Challenge Question 47: Company Picnic

```
SELECT
   N1.BusinessEntityID
   ,FullName =   CONVERT (VARCHAR (50), FirstName) + ' ' +
                 CONVERT (VARCHAR (50), LastName) + ISNULL (', ' + Suffix, '')
   ,Dept =       N4.Name
FROM Person.Person N1
INNER JOIN (SELECT
              BusinessEntityID
              ,MaxStart = MAX (StartDate)
           FROM HumanResources.EmployeeDepartmentHistory
           GROUP BY BusinessEntityID) N2
   ON N1.BusinessEntityID = N2.BusinessEntityID
INNER JOIN HumanResources.EmployeeDepartmentHistory N3
   ON N2.MaxStart = N3.StartDate AND N2.BusinessEntityID = N3.BusinessEntityID
INNER JOIN HumanResources.Department N4 ON N3.DepartmentID = N4.DepartmentID
WHERE N1.PersonType IN ('SP', 'EM')
ORDER BY Dept, FullName
```

Solution to Challenge Question 48: Sales Quota Changes

```sql
SELECT DISTINCT
   N1.BusinessEntityID
   ,SalesRepLastName =    N4.LastName
   ,Yr2006StartQuota =    N2.SalesQuota
   ,Yr2007EndQuota =      N3.SalesQuota
   ,[%ChangeQuota] =      (N3.SalesQuota - N2.SalesQuota) / N2.SalesQuota * 100
FROM Sales.SalesPersonQuotaHistory N1
INNER JOIN Sales.SalesPersonQuotaHistory N2
   ON N1.BusinessEntityID = N2.BusinessEntityID
      AND N2.QuotaDate = (SELECT MIN (QuotaDate)
                          FROM Sales.SalesPersonQuotaHistory
                          WHERE YEAR (QuotaDate) = 2006)
INNER JOIN Sales.SalesPersonQuotaHistory N3
   ON N1.BusinessEntityID = N3.BusinessEntityID
      AND N3.QuotaDate = (SELECT MAX (QuotaDate)
                          FROM Sales.SalesPersonQuotaHistory
                          WHERE YEAR (QuotaDate) = 2007)
INNER JOIN Person.Person AS N4
   ON N1.BusinessEntityID = N4.BusinessEntityID
```

Solution to Challenge Question 49: Scrap Rate

```sql
--DROP VIEW Production.Vw_ScrapRates

CREATE VIEW Production.Vw_ScrapRates

AS

SELECT TOP 10 PERCENT
   N1.WorkOrderID
   ,DueDate =          CAST (N1.DueDate AS DATE)
   ,ProdName =         N3.Name
   ,ScrapReason =      N2.Name
   ,N1.ScrappedQty
   ,N1.OrderQty
   ,[PercScrapped] =   ROUND (N1.ScrappedQty / CONVERT (FLOAT, N1.OrderQty)* 100, 2)
FROM Production.WorkOrder N1
INNER JOIN Production.ScrapReason N2 ON N1.ScrapReasonID = N2.ScrapReasonID
INNER JOIN Production.Product N3 ON N1.ProductID = N3.ProductID
WHERE N1.ScrappedQty / CONVERT (FLOAT, N1.OrderQty) > 0.03
ORDER BY N1.DueDate DESC
```

Solution to Challenge Question 50: Reasons

```sql
WITH Reasons AS
    (SELECT
        N1.SalesOrderID
        ,ReasonName =      N2.Name

        ,ReasonInfluence = CASE
                                WHEN COUNT (N3.SalesOrderID) > 1
                                    THEN 'Contributing Reason'
                                WHEN COUNT (N3.SalesOrderID) = 1
                                    THEN 'Exclusive Reason'
                           END
     FROM Sales.SalesOrderHeaderSalesReason N1
     INNER JOIN Sales.SalesReason N2
        ON N1.SalesReasonID = N2.SalesReasonID
     INNER JOIN Sales.SalesOrderHeaderSalesReason N3
        ON N1.SalesOrderID = N3.SalesOrderID
     GROUP BY N1.SalesOrderID, N2.Name)

SELECT
    ReasonName
    ,ReasonInfluence
    ,SalesOrderCount = COUNT (*)
FROM Reasons
GROUP BY ReasonName, ReasonInfluence
ORDER BY ReasonName, SalesOrderCount DESC
```

Solution to Challenge Question 51: Excess Inventory

```sql
-- Part I
SELECT
   SpecialOfferID
   ,DiscountType  =    [Type]
   ,DiscountDescr =    [Description]
   ,Category
   ,StartDate
   ,EndDate
   ,DiscountPct
FROM Sales.SpecialOffer
WHERE [Type] = 'Excess Inventory'

-- Part II
SELECT
   N1.SpecialOfferID
   ,DiscountType  =    [Type]
   ,DiscountDescr =    [Description]
   ,N1.Category
   ,N1.StartDate
   ,N1.EndDate
   ,N1.DiscountPct
   ,SalesOrders  =     (SELECT COUNT (DISTINCT X1.SalesOrderID)
                        FROM Sales.SalesOrderDetail X1
                        WHERE N1.SpecialOfferID = X1.SpecialOfferID)
FROM Sales.SpecialOffer N1
WHERE N1.[Type] = 'Excess Inventory'
```

Solution 1 to Challenge Question 52: Pay Rate Changes

```sql
WITH Data AS
   (SELECT
      BusinessEntityID
      ,PayRateNumber = ROW_NUMBER () OVER (PARTITION BY BusinessEntityID
                                           ORDER BY RateChangeDate DESC)
      ,RateChangeDate
      ,Rate
   FROM HumanResources.EmployeePayHistory)

SELECT
   N1.BusinessEntityID
   ,RatePrior    =    N2.Rate
   ,LatestRate   =    N1.Rate
   ,PercentChange =   CONVERT (VARCHAR (10),
                      (N1.Rate - N2.Rate) / N2.Rate * 100) + '%'
FROM Data N1
LEFT JOIN Data N2
   ON N1.BusinessEntityID = N2.BusinessEntityID AND N2.PayRateNumber = 2
WHERE N1.PayRateNumber = 1
```

Solution 2 to Challenge Question 52: Pay Rate Changes

```sql
WITH [Data] AS
(SELECT
   BusinessEntityID
   ,RateChangeDate
   ,Rate_Prior =
        LAG (Rate, 1) OVER
                    (PARTITION BY BusinessEntityID
                     ORDER BY RateChangeDate)
   ,Current_Rate =
        LAST_VALUE (Rate) OVER
                    (PARTITION BY BusinessEntityID
                     ORDER BY RateChangeDate
                     RANGE BETWEEN CURRENT ROW AND UNBOUNDED FOLLOWING)
FROM HumanResources.EmployeePayHistory N1)

SELECT
   BusinessEntityID
   ,Rate_Prior
   ,Current_Rate
   ,PercentChange =
        CONVERT (VARCHAR (10),
            ((Current_Rate - Rate_Prior)/ Rate_Prior) * 100) + '%'
FROM [Data]
WHERE RateChangeDate = (SELECT MAX (RateChangeDate)
                        FROM HumanResources.EmployeePayHistory AS X1
                        WHERE [Data].BusinessEntityID = X1.BusinessEntityID)
```

Solution 1 to Challenge Question 53: Sales Order Counts

```sql
WITH Orders AS

(SELECT
   N2.LastName
   ,FY = 'FY' + CONVERT (CHAR (4), YEAR (DATEADD (MONTH, 6, (OrderDate))))
   ,SalesOrderID
FROM Sales.SalesOrderHeader N1
INNER JOIN Person.Person AS N2 ON N1.SalesPersonID = N2.BusinessEntityID
WHERE OnlineOrderFlag = 0)

SELECT X1.LastName, X1.FY2006, X1.FY2007, X1.FY2008
FROM Orders
PIVOT (COUNT (Orders.SalesOrderID)
   FOR FY IN (FY2006, FY2007, FY2008)) X1
ORDER BY LastName
```

Solution 2 to Challenge Question 53: Sales Order Counts

```
SELECT
   N2.LastName
   ,FY2006 =
      SUM (CASE WHEN YEAR (DATEADD (MONTH, 6, (OrderDate))) = 2006 THEN 1 ELSE 0 END)
   ,FY2007 =
      SUM (CASE WHEN YEAR (DATEADD (MONTH, 6, (OrderDate))) = 2007 THEN 1 ELSE 0 END)
   ,FY2008 =
      SUM (CASE WHEN YEAR (DATEADD (MONTH, 6, (OrderDate))) = 2008 THEN 1 ELSE 0 END)
FROM Sales.SalesOrderHeader N1
INNER JOIN Person.Person AS N2 ON N1.SalesPersonID = N2.BusinessEntityID
WHERE OnlineOrderFlag = 0
GROUP BY N2.LastName
ORDER BY LastName
```

Solution to Challenge Question 54: Loyal Customers

```
-- Part I
SELECT
   LoyalCustomers =     COUNT (*)
   ,TotalCustomers =    (SELECT COUNT (DISTINCT CustomerID)
                         FROM Sales.SalesOrderHeader
                         WHERE SalesPersonID IS NOT NULL)
FROM (SELECT CustomerID
      FROM Sales.SalesOrderHeader
      WHERE SalesPersonID IS NOT NULL
      GROUP BY CustomerID
      HAVING COUNT (*) >= 10
         AND COUNT (DISTINCT SalesPersonID) = 1) X1

-- Part II
DECLARE @CustomerID INT =
   (SELECT TOP 1 CustomerID
    FROM (SELECT CustomerID
          FROM Sales.SalesOrderHeader N1
          WHERE SalesPersonID IS NOT NULL
          GROUP BY N1.CustomerID
          HAVING COUNT (*) >= 10
             AND COUNT (DISTINCT SalesPersonID) = 1) X1
ORDER BY NEWID ())

SELECT *
FROM Sales.SalesOrderHeader
WHERE CustomerID = @CustomerID
```

Solution to Challenge Question 55: Date Range Gaps

```
WITH [Data] AS

(SELECT
   ProductID
   ,StartDate
   ,EndDate
   ,Days_to_Next_Start =
       ISNULL (DATEDIFF (DAY, EndDate,
           LEAD (StartDate) OVER (PARTITION BY ProductID ORDER BY StartDate)), 0)
FROM Production.ProductListPriceHistory)

SELECT ProductID
FROM [Data]
WHERE Days_to_Next_Start > 1

-- No date range gaps exist.
```

INDEX

Aggregate formulas
    AVG 62, 63, 77, 83, 88
    COUNT 2, 55, 56, 60, 61, 62, 64, 66, 69, 72, 74, 76, 77, 78, 81, 84, 85, 87, 92, 93, 95, 96
    MAX 56, 62, 63, 64, 67, 68, 78, 79, 81, 88, 89, 90, 91
    MIN 62, 63, 68, 88, 91
    SUM 50, 51, 53, 54, 55, 56, 57, 60, 64, 65, 66, 73, 75, 76, 77, 79, 80, 83, 85, 86, 87, 88, 96
BETWEEN 55, 75, 87, 88
Case statements 1, 52, 60, 62, 64, 66, 68, 72, 76, 77, 78, 84, 85, 86, 92, 96
CAST 54, 55, 56, 91
Challenge questions
    Advanced 11, 12, 31, 32, 36
    Beginner 6, 8, 9, 12, 14, 19, 20, 22, 24, 28, 32
    Intermediate 3, 4, 5, 7, 10, 12, 13, 14, 15, 16, 17, 18, 19, 20, 21, 23, 24, 25, 26, 27, 29, 30, 33, 34, 35, 37
Common table expressions (CTE) 51, 55, 58, 59, 63, 64, 67, 69, 72, 73, 85, 92, 94, 95, 97
CONVERT 54, 60, 62, 64, 66, 77, 81, 82, 83, 87, 90, 91, 94, 95
CREATE TABLE 86
Date formulas
    DATEADD 50, 51, 52, 54, 55, 73, 83, 86, 95, 96
    DATEDIFF 67, 75, 77, 78, 86, 97
    DATEFROMPARTS 56
    DATENAME 55, 86
    DATEPART 50, 51, 52, 55
    DAY 75, 97
    EOMONTH 56, 75
    MONTH 50, 51, 52, 54, 55, 77, 95, 96
    QUARTER 50, 51
    WEEKDAY 55
    YEAR 50, 51, 52, 54, 55, 63, 65, 70, 73, 79, 80, 83, 84, 85, 86, 91, 96
DECLARE 59, 60, 75, 86, 96
DENSE_RANK 68, 73
Derived Table 77, 96
DISTINCT 2, 56, 60, 61, 63, 64, 76, 81, 91, 93, 96
Downloads
    AdventureWorks2012 x
    Solution files x
    SQL Server x
EXCEPT 58
GROUP BY .. 2, 50, 51, 53, 54, 55, 56, 57, 60, 61, 62, 63, 64, 65, 66, 67, 68, 69, 72, 73, 74, 76, 77, 78, 79, 80, 81, 82, 83, 84, 85, 86, 87, 88, 90, 92, 96
    HAVING 2, 60, 80, 81, 96
INSERT INTO 86
ISNULL 1, 59, 87, 88, 90, 97
ISNUMERIC 76

Joins
- INNER JOIN ... 50, 51, 52, 54, 57, 58, 59, 60, 62, 63, 64, 65, 67, 68, 69, 70, 71, 73, 74, 76, 78, 79, 80, 82, 85, 87, 89, 90, 91, 92, 95, 96
- LEFT JOIN ... 1, 50, 56, 57, 71, 72, 83, 88, 94

LAG ... 51, 95
LAST_VALUE ... 95
LEAD ... 97
LIKE ... 1, 71, 85
Median calculations ... 62, 63
NEWID ... 79, 96
NOT EXISTS ... 58
NTILE ... 77
ORDER BY .1, 50, 51, 54, 55, 56, 59, 61, 62, 63, 65, 66, 67, 68, 69, 71, 72, 73, 74, 75, 76, 77, 79, 80, 81, 82, 83, 84, 85, 86, 87, 89, 90, 91, 92, 94, 95, 96
Percent calculations ... 50, 60, 66, 77, 81, 82, 83, 91, 94, 95
PERCENTILE_DISC ... 63
PIVOT ... 61, 95
ROUND ... 66, 77, 91
ROW_NUMBER ... 54, 55, 62, 69, 85, 87, 94
Running totals ... 55
SET ... 54, 62, 81, 86, 87
String formulas
- CHARINDEX ... 75
- LEFT ... 75
- LEN ... 75
- RIGHT ... 64, 75

Subquery ... 54, 56, 57, 58, 59, 60, 61, 62, 78, 79, 81, 87, 89, 90, 91, 93, 95, 96
Temporary tables ... 1, 50, 51, 52, 54, 56, 60, 61, 62, 80, 81, 83, 87, 88
TOP ... 54, 55, 59, 81, 87, 89, 91, 96
UNION ... 55
UPDATE ... 54, 62, 81, 86, 87
USE ... 1
VIEW ... 64, 79, 91
WHILE ... 86
WITH ROLLUP ... 64

Printed in Great Britain
by Amazon